Best Wishes '52

To Mrs Ruth ~~Stone~~ Danby

from E. Cashdan

GW00545883

THE BOOK OF PSALMS
SEFER TEHILLIM

translated into English by
Rabbi Eli Cashdan

MINERVA PRESS
MONTREUX LONDON WASHINGTON

THE BOOK OF PSALMS (*SEFER TEHILLIM*)
Copyright © Rabbi Eli Cashdan 1997

All Rights Reserved

No part of this book may be reproduced in any form,
by photocopying or by any electronic or mechanical means,
including information storage or retrieval systems,
without permission in writing from both the copyright owner
and the publisher of this book.

ISBN 1 86106 324 5

First Published 1997 by
MINERVA PRESS
195 Knightsbridge
London SW7 1RE

Printed in Great Britain by
Antony Rowe Ltd, Chippenham, Wiltshire

THE BOOK OF PSALMS
SEFER TEHILLIM

Foreword

The Book of Psalms is the great lexicon of human spirituality. In its verses, generations have found consummate expression of the entire range of religious emotions, from penitence to joy, despair to hope, humility to exaltation. As C. H. Cornhill wrote a century ago, 'The Psalms resound, and will continue to resound, as long as there shall be men created in the image of God, in whose hearts the sacred fire of religion shines and glows; for they are religion itself put into speech.'

Small wonder then that *Sefer Tehillim*, as the book is known in Hebrew, occupies so large a place in Jewish liturgy and that it was to Psalms more than any other single source that Jews – and not only Jews – turned to give voice to their public and private prayers.

Every age needs its own translations to make the work accessible, and in Eli Cashdan it has found a masterly translator. In a unique scholarly career spanning some sixty years, he has taught and inspired many of Anglo-Jewry's spiritual leaders. His translations range from early contributions to the Soncino *Talmud* to the more recent and outstanding English rendition of the *Authorised Daily Prayer Book*. This new English version of the Psalms has all the qualities that we have come to associate with his work. Simple, direct, lucid and intelligible, informed not only by previous translations but also by the classic Jewish commentaries, it will allow these masterpieces of religious poetry to speak with their ageless power to a new generation.

Judaism is not a religion of systematic theology. We sing our faith rather than analyse it. Perhaps that is the secret of the Psalms. They are language on the brink of music, from brooding chamber works like 'Out of the depths I call to You, O LORD' (Psalm 130) to the great choral symphony of Psalms 145 to 150, which form the prelude to our daily morning prayers. They are songs, some dark, others blazing with light, of the soul in conversation with God. Their tonality is marked, in Robert Alter's phrase, by 'a kind of luminous immediacy in the apprehension of the world through the eyes of faith'.

Religious language has never before or since had quite this combination of simplicity, subtlety and emotional range. Therein lies the greatness of the Psalms, for they express in unsurpassed words and images the music of the human spirit as it reaches beyond itself to God.

We need them today. Too often we find ourselves inarticulate in the face of tragedy and triumph, crisis and thanksgiving. The English language has lost much of its grandeur since the days when every schoolchild knew the words of "The LORD is my shepherd, I shall not want" (Psalm 23) or "I lift my eyes to the mountains; from where will my help come?" (Psalm 121). Our anxieties have not diminished. Our hopes are no less strong. But we have lost that intimate familiarity with the great words which gave shape to our feelings and placed them in the context of a great religious tradition. We are indebted to Eli Cashdan for allowing us to encounter the Psalms anew, to understand them better and to make them once again the language of the heart.

Chief Rabbi Dr Jonathan Sacks
Iyar 5756/May 1996

Preface

The Book of Psalms, *Sefer Tehillim*, enjoys a special distinction among the Books of the Bible. Next to the Five Books of Moses, the Book of Psalms was the most popular reading among the Jews. With the *Tehillim* in his hand the Jew felt that he had a true companion and guide throughout life. It taught him how to pray; it offered him comfort and faith in misfortune; it gave him light in darkness.

Unfortunately, for many centuries the Hebrew language was a stranger to the Jewish mind, and the reading of the Psalms became an exercise learned by rote, without meaning or understanding. The Psalms were provided with commentaries, with notes and interpretation, but the rhythm, the swing and cadences of the original were lacking. Then translations were resorted to; and the number of translations into the language of the land is legion. Translations, however, have their shortcomings as the original language has many unusual idioms which make the task of translating difficult and, very frequently, a challenge to the translator.

Many years I spent in producing this new translation into English. My whole purpose was to provide a simple and meaningful translation into modern English, and to clarify many passages which, in earlier versions, have been difficult to understand. To arrive at the true meaning of a phrase and the sense of a verse I have resorted to previous translations and commentaries, written in Hebrew as well as in secular language. I have researched in early and medieval commentaries. I made constant use of the outstanding Hebrew commentaries of Rashi (Rabbi Solomon Ben Isaac, 1040-1105 CE), Abraham ibn Ezra (1089-1164 CE) and Radak (Rabbi David Kimhi, 1160-1235 CE) and many others. I learned much from the notable translations into English, from the Authorised Version (1611) to the most recent Revised English Bible (1989), and from the numerous English commentaries to the Psalms.

I must point out several features in the present translation. I have avoided the archaisms and obsolete words and phrases found so frequently in the earlier translations. The traditional text of the Hebrew Bible, i.e. the Masoretic text, has been followed throughout, and all the emendations suggested by scholars have been avoided. The Divine Name is always rendered the LORD, all in capitals. The 'thou' form of address to God which was commonly used in the past, has been abandoned and with it the strange verbal forms such as 'didst' and 'liveth' have gone too. 'You' or 'Your' and 'He' or 'His' when referring to the Deity have been adopted, but with initial capitals.

In many parts of this translation Hebrew words are left untranslated, particularly in the Psalm headings. Lengthy studies have been made on these words, but none are convincing. I have, therefore, had these words spelt out in English characters. They are listed at the end of the introduction, and the reader is directed to turn there in order to obtain some idea of the terms. I have not overloaded the page with notes and references, so as not to disturb or interrupt the flow of the words.

The pleasantest aspect of a preface is the opportunity for expressing heartfelt thanks to all who helped in the production of this translation. I am grateful to the hundreds of students who attended my lectures on the Psalms and to the many suggestions they made for the elucidation of the text.

My gratitude is extended to my late wife, Minnie Rachel, who constantly encouraged me to carry on with the work even when my spirits were flagging and other tasks claimed my time and attention.

My friends and colleagues, in particular Dr Louis Collins, were most helpful with advice and suggestions. It was the great Rabbi Judah, the compiler and editor of the Mishnah who declared: "Much have I learnt from my teachers, more from my colleagues and most from my students."

To my nephew, Mr David Cashdan, I extend my sincerest thanks for his helpfulness and enthusiasm to see this work through to publication.

Above all, I am deeply indebted to my daughter, Evelyn, without whose devotion and interest this work would never have seen the light of day. She had a great understanding of the work. She prodded me and encouraged me. Every page she typed and retyped whenever necessary, and made corrections and suggestions. If merit is given she certainly shares it with me.

May the Almighty pay due reward to all. It is my prayer that this translation be read by many, and read aloud, and thus a deeper knowledge and appreciation of this Divine Guide will move men to greater spiritual heights and achievement.

Introduction To The Psalms

Sefer Tehillim, lit. the Book of Praises, the Hebrew title of what is commonly known as the Book of Psalms, or the Psalter, is a collection of religious poems without parallel in any literature. It contains 150 poems, usually grouped into five books, each group being marked off by a concluding doxology, a shout of praise to God. The last verse of each book is the doxology, while Psalm 150 is the final doxology of the entire Book of Psalms. The five books are as follows: Book 1: 1-41, Book II: 42-72, Book III: 73-89, Book IV: 90-106, Book V: 107-150.

The Book of Psalms is the hymn book and prayer book of the Jewish people. It is the deposit of the religious soul of Israel, and of the religious experience of individual Israelites. There is no type of religious experience that is not mirrored forth in the Psalms.

The Book of Psalms possesses certain features which sets it apart from the rest of the Bible. All the books of the Bible are God's teaching, revealing the Divine message to man. This is true of the Torah and of the prophetic writings. In the Book of Psalms man addresses God; his soul reaches out to God for enlightenment, grace and nearness to God. Almost on every page of the Psalms is to be found the expression of confident trust in God. The mood of gratitude is a characteristic note in the Psalms. Here we hear the soul's expression of guilt, and there we are stirred by the heart's cry for pardon. We hear shouts of love and hatred, shouts of suffering and rejoicing, shouts of faith and hope. Here a man who has suffered injury demands justice, or a sick man who has escaped death gives thanks. There we hear the laments of a defeated nation, or the petitions of a nation for the punishment of its enemies. We are introduced to the psalmist's meditation on the law of God, and his passion for the Torah. We also meet with some reflective psalms where the individual grapples with the problem of suffering. Above all, the Book of Psalms abounds in prayers both personal and national;

some portray the most intimate feelings of one person, while others represent the needs and feelings of all the people of God.

The Psalms are generally referred to as the Psalms of David, and it is usually assumed that the author was the King of Israel, noted as a skilful musician, and described as the 'sweet psalmist of Israel' (2 Sam, 23.1). The Midrash on Psalms (Ps.1) states that David gave Israel the Five Books of the Psalms, just as Moses gave them the Five Books of the Torah. Thus the impression was created that all the Psalms were ascribed to him. However, the Babylonian Talmud (Baba Bathra, 15a), in the section which treats the authorship of the various books of the Bible, informs us that David wrote the Psalms with the help of ten elders, meaning that he included in the Book of Psalms the work of these ten elders: Adam, Melchizedek, Abraham, Moses, Heman (Ethan), Jeduthun, Asaph, and the three sons of Korah. Evidently it was recognised that the Book of Psalms was a collection of composite authorship, but the entire Book was named after David by virtue of the fact that most of the individual psalms (73 psalms) bear the title *le-David*, meaning 'of, for, or by David,' or from the Davidic collection. To this basic collection of David were added psalms from the Chief Musician's or Choirmaster's collection (a total of 55 psalms), from two Levitical collections: the Asaph collection (12 psalms, nos. 50 and 73-88) and the sons of Korah collection (11 psalms, nos. 42, 44-49, 84, 85, 87, 88). Other collections are: The Songs of Ascent (15 psalms, nos. 120-134), the Hallel psalms (6 psalms, nos. 113-118), the Hallelujah psalms (10 in number, psalms 106, 111-113, 135 and 146-150), and also that long and elaborately constructed Psalm 119 (consisting of 22 strophes of eight lines each, corresponding to the 22 letters of the Hebrew alphabet) which is a hymn in praise of the Law, or of God who gave the Law.

All the Psalms bear titles or descriptive headings, with the exception of thirty-four, known as 'orphan' psalms. These titles either associate the psalm with a particular individual or group, or describe the type, character or style of the poem. Some titles indicate the purpose or usage of the psalm, some furnish liturgical or musical directions, and some name certain popular melodies or songs, to the tune of which the psalm was sung.

There is considerable uncertainty about the meaning of many of these terms. Here follows a list, in alphabetical order, of the proper names, the technical terms and the musical directions referred to in the captions.

Acrostic Psalms. Eight psalms are acrostic, that is, the initial letter of the successive verses are in alphabetical order. These Psalms are 9/10, 25, 34, 37, 111, 112, 119 and 145. The most complete is 119 where each strophe of eight verses, in the twenty-two successive strophes, follows the alphabetical scheme.

Alamoth. This term occurs only in Psalm 46 and in 1 Chronicles 15:20. The word is a transliteration of the Hebrew for 'young women'. The suggestion that it refers to 'women's voices' cannot be upheld for such did not exist in the Temple, nor would it have been allowed. From the Chronicles reference it clearly connotes a musical instrument, perhaps of a soprano pitch.

Al tashheth appears in the title of four psalms, 57-59 and 75. Literally the phrase means 'Destroy not'. It may be the name of a song beginning with these words (Ibn Ezra), or a direction to the Chief Musician to observe the strict mode of singing, and not to deviate from it.

Asaph. This name appears in the caption of Pss.50, and 73-83. In 1 Chronicles 6:24 it states that a Levite, named Asaph, was appointed by David as one of the chief musicians in the Temple. Moreover, the sons of Asaph, referred to in Nehemiah's time (Nehemiah 7:44) as singers, were a musical guild going back, no doubt, to the Asaph in David's time. The Asaph psalms may have been either composed or compiled by this guild of musicians. The Talmud tells us that Asaph was one of the ten worthies who assisted David in the compilation of the Book of Psalms.

Ascents, Songs of. The Hebrew title is *shir-hamaaloth*, meaning: songs of goings up, or of the steps, or Pilgrim songs. They form a collection of fifteen songs, Pss.120 to 134, intended for use by pilgrims when going up, or making their 'steps' to

Jerusalem. Others suggest that these psalms were sung by the exiles returning from their captivity in Babylon; see Ezra 7:9 where the term *maalah*, the singular of *maaloth*, is used in this sense. Another suggestion links the fifteen 'Songs of Ascents' with the fifteen steps leading from the Court of the Women to the Court of the Israelites, see Mishnah, *Middoth* 11:5. Furthermore, Mishnah *Sukkah*, V:4, states that on these steps the Levites stood with their musical instruments and sang their songs. These fifteen Psalms formed a separate collection of songs and were incorporated in the Book of Psalms.

Ayyeleth hashahar is found only in the title of Ps.22. Literally the phrase means: 'The hind of the dawn,' and it is generally assumed to be a cue to a popular song to whose melody the psalm was to be sung.

Chief Musician. The Hebrew term *la-menazzeah* can be rendered for the Chief Musician, or the Choirmaster, or the Leader, and it is prefixed to fifty-five psalms. It may mean directions given to the Chief Musician of the Temple orchestra or choir. Or the term might refer to a particular song taken from the Chief Musician's collection of hymns. It is a matter of surprise that this term does not occur in either Books IV or V of the Psalms. Apart from the Psalms the term is found once in Habakkuk 3:19.

Cush the Benjaminite. This historical reference is given in the title of Ps.7. There is, however, no mention of anyone of this name in the history of David; but as a Benjaminite he may have been a staunch supporter of Saul in his pursuit of David.

David. The title *le-David* (to David) is prefixed to 73 psalms. The traditional view is that it denotes authorship. But it can also mean 'belonging to David,' i.e. taken from the Davidic collection, or perhaps 'dedicated to David'. One must, however, bear in mind that the Bible itself refers to David as a musician and poet (cf. I Samuel 16:18, 2 Samuel 1:17-27.) From Amos 6:5 we learn that the name of David was connected with musical skill and the invention of musical instruments.

Ethan the Ezrahite. Psalm 89 is ascribed to Ethan, the Ezrahite, and the previous psalm, 88, to Heman, the Ezrahite. Both these men are named as levitical singers in 1 Chronicles 15:17. Both are also mentioned among the four great sages in the time of Solomon, cf. 1 Kings 5:11. Their skill probably lay in composing songs of praise for the Temple service.

Gittith. This term occurs in the titles of Pss.8, 81 and 84. The Targum connects the term with the city Gath, hence a musical instrument or melody which originated in this Philistine city. Others connect the term with the Hebrew *gath* meaning a wine press, hence a vintage melody.

Hallel. The designation 'Hallel' (songs of praise) is applied to Pss.113-118, referred to in the Talmud as the *Egyptian Hallel*, on account of the Exodus theme in the second psalm of this group. It is included in the Jewish liturgy for recital at Festivals and at New Moon. Ps.136, known as the *Great Hallel*, praises God as the controlling Power of Nature and of Israel's history. According to Mishnah *Taanith* III:9, the Great Hallel was sung on communal joyous occasions.

Hallelujah. There are ten psalms beginning with Hallelujah (Praise the LORD), which apparently formed a distinct group of psalms and were later incorporated into the Book of Psalms.

Heman the Ezrahite found only in Ps.88. See note under Ethan the Ezrahite.

Higgaion. This term is connected with the Hebrew root *hagah* 'to meditate', hence a meditative melody. It might indicate a musical flourish, during which the people would meditate on the theme of the psalm. It occurs once in Ps.9 at the conclusion of verse 17 and again in Ps.92:4.

Jeduthun appears in the titles of Pss.39, 62 and 77. This would seem to be the name of a member of a musical guild instituted by David (see 1 Chronicles 16:41,42). However, Rashi suggests that it is the name of a musical instrument.

Jonath elem rehokim occurs only in Ps.56. The Hebrew might be translated as 'the silent dove among far-off peoples'. It is doubtless the title of a song to whose melody the psalm was sung.

Korah, Sons of, found in the headings of eleven psalms (42, 44-49, 84, 85, 87, 88). The three sons of Korah, according to Rabbinic tradition, were among the worthies who collaborated with David in the production of the Book of Psalms. They were one of the leading guilds of Temple singers. See note on Asaph.

Lehazkir. Lit. 'for remembrance' or 'for the memorial offering', this term appears in the title of Pss.38 and 70. It probably means that the psalms in question were chanted while the memorial part (*azkarah*) of the sacrifice was burnt on the altar. Rashi, however, suggests that the purpose of this psalm was to 'remind' God of the distress of the people.

Mahalath appears in Ps.53. The word may mean sickness and could refer to the title of a plaintive or sombre melody to which the psalm was sung. According to Rashi, it may be the name of a musical instrument.

Mahalath le-annoth is found only in Ps.88. The second element of the title is derived from the Hebrew root *anah*, to respond, hence the suggestion that the psalm was sung antiphonally.

Maskil appears in thirteen titles. The meaning of this term is obscure but it is suggested that the word may mean a well-considered and constructed poem. In most of the psalms the title implies a reflective or meditative poem; however, in 2 Chronicles 30:22 the term clearly denotes an artistic musical performance.

Miktam is an obscure word occurring in Pss.16 and 57-60. The term
is often connected with the Hebrew *ketem*, meaning 'gold,'
hence a 'golden poem', signifying the style of the poem. The
Greek and the Targum both interpret the term as an inscribed
or engraved text, hence referring to a work of abiding worth.

Mizmor, usually translated 'Psalm', occurs in fifty-seven Psalms and
nowhere else in the Bible. It is a technical term and
invariably refers to a composition intended for
accompaniment by stringed instruments.

Moses appears only in Ps.90, although according to Rabbinic tradition
the eleven psalms 90-100 are all attributed to Moses.

Muth labben. An obscure term found only in Ps.9. Its literal
meaning might be 'on the death of the son', or 'on the death
of Labben', but it is unknown to what specific incident the
reference is made. Perhaps it is the title of an elegy to whose
melody the psalm was to be sung.

Nehiloth. Found only in the title of Ps.5; the meaning of the Hebrew
term is uncertain. It may mean 'wind instruments' derived
from the Hebrew word *halil*, a pipe or flute. Some suggest it
is the title of a song; others relate it to the Hebrew *nahil*,
meaning 'a swarm of bees' hence, instruments emitting a
buzzing sound.

Selah. This term is found seventy-one times in the Book of Psalms
and three times in the Book of Habakkuk in chap. 3: 3, 9,
and 13. In spite of the frequency the meaning is uncertain.
The Talmud, in *Erubin*, 54a states that *selah* has no other
meaning than 'forever'. This also is the view of the Targum.
According to modern views the term has no interpretative
meaning in the context of the psalm. The general opinion
seems to be that *selah* is a musical sign denoting an interlude
or a pause. The word is derived from the root *salal* meaning
'to lift up'. It may therefore be a direction to the orchestra to
play louder, or a direction to the singers to increase the

volume of their praise. Ibn Ezra suggests that the term was inserted by the author of the psalm to emphasise the theme of the passage; as if to say 'this is truly so'. But he offers no etymological basis for this explanation.

Sheminith. Lit. 'the eighth'; a musical term found in Pss.6 and 12, and in 1 Chronicles 15:21. It is possibly a stringed instrument with eight strings; cf. Ps.92:4, *asor*, an instrument with ten strings.

Shiggaion occurs only in Ps.7, and once, also, in the plural, in Habakkuk 3:1. The meaning of this term is obscure. Some relate this word to the Hebrew root denoting 'to stray, err', and explain it as a dithyramb, an irregular and emotional poem. Alternatively, it may be connected with a similar Akkadian root meaning 'to lament', hence a dirge.

Shir, a song, appears in thirty titles. It is a general title for religious and secular songs. It is often combined with the term *mizmor*, either as *mizmor shir* as in Ps.92, or as *shir mizmor* as in Ps.89; the significance of the order is unknown.

Shoshannim. Lit. 'Lilies'. This term is used in Pss.45, 69 and 80, and seems to be a direction that the psalm was to be sung to the tune of 'The Lilies', obviously a well-known song.

Shushan eduth. Lit. 'The Lily of Testimony' appears only in Ps.60. It is clearly the title of a song to whose melody the psalm was to be sung.

Solomon. This caption is found only in Pss. 72 and 127. According to Rashi Ps.72 was a prayer by David on behalf of his son, Solomon, that he rule his subjects in the spirit of justice and righteousness. As to Ps.127, the reason it is ascribed to Solomon is no doubt the view that 'the house' in verse 1 refers to the building of the Temple.

BOOK I

PSALM 1

THE TWO PATHS

1. Happy is the man
   who never follows the advice of the wicked,
   nor lingers in the path of the sinners,
   nor sits in the company of scoffers;
2. but finds his delight in the Torah of the LORD,
   and meditates in His Torah day and night.
3. He is like a tree planted beside streams of water,
   that yields fruit in season,
   and whose leaf never withers.
   He succeeds in everything he does.
4. Not so is it with the wicked.
   They are like chaff which the wind blows away.
5. Therefore, when judgement comes the wicked shall not stand
   firm, nor sinners in the company of the righteous.
6. For the LORD cares for the way of the righteous,
   but the way of the wicked is doomed.

PSALM 2

A WARNING TO KINGS AND PRINCES

1. Why do the nations rage,
   and the peoples devise futile plots?
2. Kings of the earth stand ready,
   and princes conspire together
   against the LORD and against His anointed, saying,
3. "Let us break their fetters,
   and cast off their bonds from us."
4. He who is enthroned in heaven laughs,
   the LORD mocks at them.
5. Then He speaks to them in His anger,
   and terrifies them in His wrath,
6. "I have set up My king
   on Zion, My holy mountain."

7. I will announce the decree:
   The LORD said to me, "You are My son;
   this day I have become your father.
8. Ask of Me,
   and I will give you nations as your inheritance,
   the ends of the earth as your possession.
9. You will break them with a rod of iron,
   and shatter them like a potter's jar."

10. So now, kings, be prudent;
    be warned, you rulers of the earth.
11. Serve the LORD with reverence,
    rejoice with trembling.
12. Pay homage with sincerity,
    lest He be angry and you end in ruin;*
    for His anger flares up in a moment.
    Happy are all who find refuge in Him!

---

* Lit. 'perish in the way'.

22

PSALM 3

A CRY OF A MAN IN DISTRESS

1.   A psalm of David, when he fled from his son Absalom.

2.   LORD, how many are my foes!
Many rise against me.

3.   Many are saying of me,
"There is no help for him from God."   *Selah*[*]

4.   But You, LORD, are a shield around me;
You are my glory,
You raise high my head.

5.   When I call to the LORD,
He answers me from His holy mountain.   *Selah*

6.   I lie down to rest, and I sleep,
I wake again for the LORD upholds me.

7.   I fear not the myriads of people
who have set themselves against me on every side.

8.   Arise, LORD; save me, O my God!
Strike[**] all my enemies on the cheek;
Smash[***] the teeth of the wicked.

9.   Victory comes from the LORD;
May Your blessing rest upon Your people.   *Selah*

---

[*]   For the meaning of all the italicised words used in the Psalms, particularly in the captions, see the alphabetical list given in the introduction.

[**]   These verbs, though stated in the perfect tense, often have a precative or optative meaning, particularly when preceded by a verb in the imperative. This has now been accepted by Hebrew grammarians.

[***]   *Ibid.*

23

PSALM 4

THE LORD HEARS THE CRY OF THE FAITHFUL

1. For the Chief Musician; on stringed instruments. A psalm of David.

2. Answer me when I call,
   O my righteous God.
   When I was in distress You freed me;
   now have mercy on me, and hear my prayer.

3. You men of rank, how long will you turn my glory into shame?
   How long will you love vanity,
   and seek after falsehood?   *Selah*

4. Know that the LORD has singled out the faithful for Himself.
   The LORD hears when I call to Him.

5. Fear Him; do not sin.
   Ponder on this when you rest in bed, and be silent.   *Selah*

6. Offer righteousness as your sacrifice,
   and trust in the LORD.

7. There are many who say,
   "If only we might see better times!"
   Let the light of Your face shine upon us, LORD!

8. You have put in my heart greater joy
   than others have when their corn and wine abound.

9. In peace I lie down and sleep,
   for You alone, LORD, keep me in safety.

PSALM 5

A PRAYER FOR DIVINE AID

1.   For the Chief Musician; on *nehiloth*. A psalm of David.

2.   Give ear to my words, LORD;
   pay heed to my utterance.
3.   Listen to my cry for help, my King and my God,
   for to You I pray.
4.   Morning after morning, LORD, You hear my voice,
   morning after morning I set out my plea before You
   and wait.

5.   For You are not a God who delights in wickedness;
   no evil man can be a guest of Yours.
6.   The boastful cannot stand in Your presence;
   You hate all evil-doers.
7.   You destroy all who speak lies;
   bloodthirsty and deceitful men the LORD detests.

8.   But I, through Your great love, may come into Your house,
   I bow down towards Your holy temple in awe of You.
9.   Lead me, LORD, in Your righteousness, because of my foes;
   make Your way straight before me.
10.   For there is no truth in their talk;[*]
   their mind is bent on destruction.
   Their throat is an open grave;
   they speak so smoothly with their tongue.
11.   Condemn them, God,
   let them fall by their own devices;
   cast them out for their many crimes,
   for they have rebelled against You.

---

[*]   Lit. 'mouth'.

12. But let all who take refuge in You rejoice,
    let them ever sing for joy;
    spread Your shelter over them,
    so that those who love Your name exult in You.
13. For you, LORD, will bless the righteous man;
    You will surround him with favour as with a shield.

PSALM 6

A PRAYER IN SICKNESS

1. For the Chief Musician, with instrumental music on the
    sheminith. A psalm of David.

2. LORD, do not rebuke me in Your anger;
    do not punish me in Your wrath.
3. Have pity on me, LORD, for I am weak;
    heal me, LORD, for my bones shake with terror.
4. My whole being is greatly shaken up;
    but You, LORD – how long before You act?
5. Turn, LORD, and deliver me;
    save me, because of Your love.
6. For there is no remembrance of You among the dead;
    in Sheol who praises You?

7. I am wearied with my groaning;
    every night I drench my bed with weeping,
    I melt my couch with tears.
8. My eyes are dimmed with sorrow,
    they are worn out because of all my foes.
9. Away from me, all you evil-doers,
    for the LORD has heard my weeping.
10. Yes, the LORD has heard my entreaty;
    He has listened to my prayer.
11. All my enemies will be ashamed and dismayed;
    they will turn back in sudden confusion.

PSALM 7

AN APPEAL TO GOD'S JUSTICE

1.   A *shiggaion* of David, which he sang to the LORD,
concerning Cush, a Benjaminite.

2.   LORD, my God, in You I seek refuge;
rescue me from all my pursuers and save me,

3.   lest, like a lion, they tear me apart,
and rip me to pieces, with none to rescue.

4.   LORD, my God, if I had done these things,
if there is any guilt on my hands,

5.   if I have done evil to him who was at peace with me,
– I who delivered him who without cause was my enemy –

6.   then let an enemy pursue and overtake me,
let him trample my life to the ground,
and lay my honour in the dust.   *Selah*

7.   Arise, LORD, in Your anger,
rouse Yourself in fury against my foes;
bestir Yourself on my behalf; pronounce judgement.

8.   Let the peoples assemble around You,
and for them take Your seat on high.[*]

9.   The LORD judges the peoples.
Judge me, LORD, according to my righteousness,
and according to my integrity.

10.   Let the evil of the wicked come to an end,
but establish the righteous,
You searcher of the mind and heart,
You righteous God.

11.   I rely on God who is my shield;
He saves the upright in heart.

---

[*]   i.e. preside as Judge. The verb *shubah* (return) from the root *shub* can
also have the meaning 'sit' as though from the root *yashab*, for middle
waw verbs often interchange with initial *yod* verbs. For other examples,
see Ps.23:6, and Isaiah 1:27.

12. God is a just judge;
    every day He is indignant [with the wicked].
13. If a man does not repent,
    God will sharpen His sword,
    He will bend His bow and take aim.
14. He has prepared for him His deadly weapons,
    He has made ready His arrows
    for the pursuers [of the righteous].*

15. See, how the wicked conceives evil, is pregnant with
    mischief, and gives birth to lies.
16. He digs a pit and digs it deep,
    but he himself will fall into the hole he has made.
17. His mischief will recoil upon his own head,
    his violence will come down upon his skull.

18. I will praise the LORD for His righteousness,
    and sing psalms to the name of the LORD Most High.

---

* Following Rashi's interpretation.

29

PSALM 8

GOD'S GLORY AND MAN'S DIGNITY

1.   For the Chief Musician; on the *gittith*. A psalm of David.

2.   LORD, our Sovereign,
   how glorious is Your name in all the earth!
   Your splendour is praised as high as the heavens!

3.   Out of the mouths of infants and babes
   You have given proof of Your power,
   because of Your foes,
   to silence the enemy and the avenger.

4.   When I look up at Your heavens, the work of Your fingers,
   at the moon and the stars that You set in place,

5.   what is man that You should be mindful of him,
   a mere human, that You should take notice of him?

6.   Yet You made him little less than divine,
   and crowned him with glory and honour.

7.   You made him master over all Your handiwork,
   and put everything under his feet:

8.   sheep and oxen, all of them,
   and also the wild beasts;

9.   the birds of the heaven, the fish in the sea,
   all that swim along the ocean paths.

10.   LORD, our Sovereign,
    how glorious is Your name in all the earth!

PSALM 9

THANKSGIVING ON THE OVERTHROW
OF THE HOSTILE NATIONS

1. For the Chief Musician, set to *muth labben*. A psalm of David.

2. I will praise You, LORD, with all my heart;
I will recount all Your wonderful deeds.

3. I will rejoice and exult in You,
I will sing praise to Your name, O Most High,

4. because my enemies turn back,
they stumble and perish before You.

5. For You uphold my right and my cause,
You sit on Your throne as a righteous judge.

6. You have rebuked the nations,
You have destroyed the wicked,
You have blotted out their name for ever.

7. The enemy is finished,
in ruins for ever.
You uprooted their cities;
all memory of them is gone.

8. But the LORD abides for ever;
He has established His throne for judgement.

9. He will judge the world with justice;
He will rule the people with fairness.

10. The LORD is a tower of strength for the oppressed,
a tower of strength in times of trouble.

11. Let those who acknowledge Your name put their trust in
You, for You, LORD, do not abandon those who seek You.

12. Sing praises to the LORD who dwells in Zion;
declare His deeds among the peoples.

13. For the avenger of blood remembers,
He does not ignore the cry of the afflicted.

14. Have pity on me, LORD;
     see how I am afflicted by my foes.
     Raise me from the gates of death,

15. so that I may tell all Your praise;
     in the gates of the daughter of Zion,
     I will exult in Your deliverance.

16. The nations are sunk in the pit they made,
     their foot has been caught in the net they hid.

17. The LORD makes Himself known by the justice He does;
     the wicked man is trapped by his own devices.

                                        Higgaion Selah

18. The wicked shall go to Sheol,
     all the nations who forget God.

19. But the needy will not always be forgotten,
     nor the hope of the poor be lost for ever.

20. Arise, LORD, let no man prevail;
     let the nations be judged in Your presence.

21. Strike them with terror, LORD;
     let the nations know that they are but men.   *Selah*

PSALM 10

A PRAYER FOR HELP AGAINST OPPRESSORS

1. Why, LORD, do You stand far off,
   hiding Yourself in times of trouble?

2. The wicked in their arrogance hunt down the poor;
   may they themselves be caught in the schemes they devise!

3. The wicked man boasts of his heart's desires;
   greedy for gain, he curses and reviles the LORD.

4. The wicked man in his pride does not seek God;
   there is no room for God in all his schemes.

5. His ways prosper at all times;
   Your judgements are above and beyond his grasp;
   he snaps his fingers at all who oppose him.

6. He thinks in his heart: I shall not be shaken;
   never shall I find myself in trouble.

7. His mouth is full of curses, deceit and violence;
   mischief and evil are under his tongue.

8. He waits in ambush in the villages,
   he murders the innocent by stealth;
   his eyes are on the lookout for the hapless victims.

9. He lurks in hiding like a lion in its lair,
   he lies in wait to seize the poor;
   he seizes him and drags him away in his net.

10. He crouches, he stoops,
    and the hapless fall into his strong grip.

11. He says to himself, "God has forgotten,
    He has hidden His face, He never looks."

12. Arise, LORD; lift up Your hand for action, O God;
    do not forget the lowly.

13. Why should the wicked man revile You, God,
    and think in his heart that You will not call to account?

14.   But You see it all;
        You note mischief and grief;
        You will take the matter in hand.
        The hapless victim commits himself to You;
        You have always been the helper of the fatherless.

15.   Break the power of the wicked and evil man;
        search out his wickedness until You find no more.

16.   The LORD is King for ever and ever;
        the nations will perish from His land.

17.   You hear, LORD, the yearning of the humble;
        strengthen their hearts, and pay heed to them;

18.   do justice to the fatherless and the downtrodden,
        so that mortal man may never again inspire terror.

PSALM 11

UNSHAKEN CONFIDENCE IN GOD

1.   For the Chief Musician. Of David.

    In the LORD I take refuge.
    How then can you say to me:
    "Flee like a bird to your mountain.
2.   For look, the wicked are bending the bow,
    they are fitting their arrows to the string,
    to shoot from the darkness at the upright."
3.   When the foundations are undermined,
    what can the righteous man do?

4.   The LORD is in His holy temple,
    the LORD has His throne in heaven.
    Yet His eyes look down [on the world],
    His gaze* examines the sons of man.
5.   The LORD examines the righteous;
    but despises the wicked and the lover of violence.
6.   He will rain down upon the wicked
    flaming coals and brimstone;
    a scorching wind will be their allotted portion.
7.   For the LORD is righteous;
    He loves righteous deeds;
    the upright shall see His face.

---

*   Lit. 'His eyelids'.

PSALM 12

A PRAYER AGAINST A DECEITFUL WORLD

1. For the Chief Musician, on the *sheminith*. A psalm of David.

2. Help, LORD, for the devout are no more;
    the faithful have vanished from among men.

3. Men speak lies to one another,
    they talk with flattering lips and double minds.

4. May the LORD cut off all flattering lips,
    every boastful tongue!

5. They say, "With our tongue we shall prevail,
    our lips are our own; who is lord over us?"

6. "Because of the oppression of the poor
    and the groans of the needy,
    I will now arise," says the LORD;
    "I will give help," He assures him.*

7. The words of the LORD are pure words,
    like silver refined in an earthen crucible,
    purified seven times over.

8. You, LORD, will guard them.
    You will protect each one from such people for ever.

9. On every side the wicked strut freely
    when vileness is rated high among men.

---

*   So all Jewish commentators. Others: 'I will give him the help for
    which he longs.'

36

PSALM 13

THE PRAYER OF A MAN IN SORROW

1.   For the Chief Musician. A psalm of David.

2.   How long, LORD? Will You forget me for ever?
   How long will You hide Your face from me?
3.   How long must I bear anxieties in my mind,
   grief in my heart day after day?
   How long shall my enemy exalt himself over me?
4.   Look now, and answer me, LORD my God!
   Give light to my eyes, lest I sleep the sleep of death;
5.   lest my enemy says: "I have overcome him;"
   lest my foes rejoice when I fall.
6.   But I trust in Your loving-kindness,
   my heart rejoices in Your deliverance.
   I will sing to the LORD
   for He has been good to me.

PSALM 14

THE FATE OF THE UNGODLY

1. For the Chief Musician. Of David.

    The senseless man says in his heart,
    "There is no God."
    All are corrupt, they do abominable acts;
    there is no one who does good.
2. The LORD looks down from heaven on mankind
    to see if there are any who act wisely,
    any who seek God.
3. But they all have gone astray,
    they are all equally rotten;
    there is no one who does good,
    not even one.
4. Will all these evil-doers never learn,
    who devour My people as men eat bread,
    and never call upon the LORD?
5. There they are, in terror and in dread;
    for God is with the righteous generation.
6. You would confound the plans of the poor,
    but the LORD is his refuge.
7. O that the deliverance of Israel might come from Zion!
    When the LORD restores the fortunes of His people,
    Jacob will rejoice, Israel will be glad.

PSALM 15

THE GUEST OF GOD

1. LORD, who may dwell in Your tent?
   Who may live on Your holy mountain?
2. One whose life is blameless,
   who does what is right,
   and speaks the truth from his heart;
3. who does not slander with his tongue,
   who never wrongs his fellow,
   and casts no slur on his neighbour;
4. who has nothing but contempt for a vile man,
   but honours those who fear the LORD;
   who holds to his oath even to his own hurt;
5. who does not lend his money at interest,
   and accepts no bribe against the innocent.
   The man who does this will never be shaken.

PSALM 16

WHO IS THE FRIEND OF GOD?

1.   A *miktam* of David.

        Guard me, God, for I seek refuge in You.
2.   I say to the LORD, "You are my Master."
        You are not bound to promote my welfare;*
3.   but [You do so] on account of the holy ones
        who were in the land,
        and the noble men, in whom was all my delight.
4.   Many shall be the sorrows of those who woo another god.
        Never will I offer libations of blood to such gods;
        never will I take their names upon my lips.
5.   The LORD alone is my portion, my share, my cup of destiny;
        You hold my lot secure.
6.   A measured portion has fallen for me in delightful places;
        excellent indeed is my heritage.
7.   I will bless the LORD who gives me counsel;
        at night my thoughts instruct me.
8.   I set the LORD before me always;
        with Him at my right hand I shall not falter.
9.   Therefore my heart is glad, my soul rejoices,
        my whole body is secure and at rest.
10.   For You will not abandon my soul to the grave,
        nor suffer Your faithful servant to see the pit.
11.   You will make known to me the path of life;
        in Your presence is fullness of joy,
        at Your right hand bliss for evermore.

---

*   Following Rashi; cf. Talmud Menahot, 53a.

PSALM 17

THE INNOCENT MAN PLEADS HIS CAUSE

1. A prayer of David.

   Hear, LORD, my just cause, listen to my cry.
   Give ear to my prayer from lips without deceit.
2. Let my judgement come forth from You;
   let Your eyes discern what is right.
3. Were You to test my heart, and watch me all night long,
   were You to try me [as in a furnace],
   You would find no evil in me.
   I have resolved that my mouth should not transgress.
4. With regard to man's activities –
   being mindful of the command of Your lips,
   I have kept myself from the ways of the lawless.
5. My steps have held firmly to Your paths,
   my feet have never faltered.

6. I call on You, for You will answer me, God.
   Turn Your ear to me; listen to my words.
7. Display Your wonderful love,
   You who save with Your right hand
   those who seek refuge from attackers.
8. Guard me like the apple of Your eye;
   hide me in the shadow of Your wings
9. from the wicked who do me violence,
   from my deadly enemies who encircle me.
10. They close their hearts to pity,
    their mouths speak nothing but arrogance.
11. [They track] our steps; now they surround us;
    they set their eyes to throw us to the ground.
12. They are like a lion hungry for prey,
    like a young lion crouching in ambush.

13. Arise, LORD, confront them, bring them down;
    save my life from the wicked by Your sword.
14. By Your hand, LORD, [rescue me] from such men –
    men whose portion in life is of this world.
    But as for Your treasured people,
    fill their bellies with every good;
    may their sons have plenty,
    and have something to leave for their offspring.
15. Then I, in righteousness, will behold Your face;
    when I awake, I shall be content with the vision of You.

PSALM 18

DAVID'S SONG OF VICTORY

1.   For the Chief Musician. Of David the servant of the LORD,
     who recited to the LORD the words of this song when the
     LORD had saved him from the hands of all his enemies and
     from the hand of Saul.

2.   He said:
     I love You, LORD, my strength.
3.   The LORD is my rock, my fortress, my deliverer,
     my God, my stronghold in whom I take refuge,
     my shield, the power of my salvation, my strong tower.
4.   I call on the LORD to whom all praise is due,
     and I am saved from my enemies.
5.   The bonds of death entangled me,
     torrents of destruction overwhelmed me;
6.   the bonds of Sheol encircled me,
     the snares of death confronted me.
7.   In my distress I called to the LORD,
     I cried to my God for help.
     From His temple He heard my voice;
     my cry to Him reached His ears.
8.   The earth reeled and rocked,
     the foundations of the mountains shook;
     they reeled, because He was angry.
9.   Smoke rose from His nostrils,
     a devouring fire from His mouth,
     that kindled coals into flame.
10. He bent the sky and came down,
     a dark cloud lay under His feet.
11. He mounted a cherub and flew,
     He soared on the wings of the wind.
12. He made darkness His screen;
     the dark rain-clouds of the sky
     were His canopy around Him.

13. The radiance of His presence pierced the clouds,
    flashing fiery hail like blazing coals.

14. The LORD thundered from heaven,
    the Most High raised His voice,
    amidst a storm of hailstones and fiery coals.

15. He shot His arrows and scattered [His foes];
    He hurled lightning bolts and routed them.

16. The ocean bed was revealed,
    the foundations of the world were laid bare,
    at Your rebuke, LORD,
    at the blast of the breath of Your nostrils.

17. From on high He reached down and took me;
    He drew me out of the mighty waters.

18. He rescued me from my powerful enemy,
    from my foes who were too strong for me.

19. They confronted me in the day of my calamity,
    but the LORD was my support.

20. He brought me out into freedom;
    He saved me because He was pleased with me.

21. The LORD rewarded me according to my merit,
    He requited me because my hands were clean.*

22. For I kept the ways of the LORD,
    and was not disloyal to my God.

23. All His laws are ever before me;
    I have not disregarded His precepts.

24. I have always been blameless before Him,
    and have kept myself from sin.

25. The LORD requited me according to my merit,
    because my hands were clean** in His sight.

26. To the loyal You show Yourself loyal,
    and to the blameless You show Yourself blameless.

27. To the sincere You show Yourself sincere,
    but to the perverse You show Yourself shrewd.

---

*   Lit. 'according to the cleanness of my hands.'
**   *Ibid.*

28. For You save the lowly people,
    but humble haughty eyes.
29. For You keep my lamp alight;
    the LORD, my God, lightens my darkness.
30. With Your help I can advance against a troop;
    with my God's aid I can scale a wall.
31. The way of God is perfect!
    The LORD's word is flawless.
    He is a shield to all who seek refuge in Him.
32. What god is there except the LORD?
    What rock but our God?
33. He is the God who girds me with strength,
    and makes my way straight.
34. He makes my feet swift as a deer,
    and sets me secure on the heights.
35. He trains my hands for battle,
    so that my arms can bend a bow of bronze.
36. You have given me Your shield of protection;
    Your right hand sustains me;
    for it is Your purpose* to make me great.
37. You made room for my steps;
    my feet have not slipped.
38. I pursue my enemies and overtake them;
    I do not turn back until I have made an end of them.
39. I strike them down and they can rise no more;
    they lie fallen at my feet.
40. You have girded me with strength for battle;
    You subdued my assailants before me.
41. You made my enemies turn their backs in flight;
    those who hated me I destroyed.
42. They cried out, but there was no one to save them;
    they cried to the LORD, but He did not answer them.
43. I crushed them fine as dust before the wind;
    I poured them out like mud in the streets.
44. You delivered me from the attacks of the people;
    You have set me at the head of nations;
    peoples I know not serve me.

---

* Or you stoop down.

45. As soon as they hear of me, they obey me;
    foreigners cringe before me.
46. Foreign people are disheartened,
    they come trembling out of their strongholds.

47. The LORD lives! Blessed is my rock!
    Exalted be God, my deliverer!
48. He is the God who vindicates me,*
    who subdues nations under me;
49. who rescues me from my enemies.
    You raise me above my foes,
    and deliver me from violent men.
50. Therefore, LORD, I will praise You among the nations,
    and sing psalms to Your name.
51. He gives great victories to His king,
    He shows loving-kindness to His anointed,
    to David and his descendants for ever.

---

* Lit. 'grants me vengeance'.

PSALM 19

GOD'S GLORY IN THE HEAVENS AND IN THE LAW

1.   For the Chief Musician. A psalm of David.

2.   The heavens declare the glory of God,
        the sky proclaims the work of His hand.
3.   Day after day they* tell their tale,
        night after night they proclaim this fact.
4.   No word, no utterance, no sound is heard,
5.   yet their message goes out through all the earth,
        and what they tell reaches to the end of the world.

        In them He has set up a tent for the sun.
6.   It comes out like a bridegroom from his chamber,
        rejoicing like a champion to run its course.
7.   It rises at one end of the heaven,
        and makes its circuit to the other end;
        and nothing is hidden from its heat.

8.   The law of the LORD is perfect,
        refreshing the soul;
        the decrees of the LORD are trustworthy,
        making wise the simple.
9.   The precepts of the LORD are right,
        giving joy to the heart;
        the commandment of the LORD is clear,
        giving light to the eyes.
10.   The fear of the LORD is pure,
        enduring for ever;
        the judgements of the LORD are true,
        righteous altogether.

---

*   i.e. the heavens.

11. They are more desirable than gold, than much fine gold;
    they are sweeter than honey, than the drippings from the
    comb.

12. By them Your servant is enlightened;*
    in keeping them there is great reward.

13. But who can be aware of errors?
    Cleanse me of hidden faults.

14. Above all, restrain Your servant from wilful sins;
    let them not rule over me,
    then shall I be blameless, innocent of great transgression.

15. May the words of my mouth, and the thoughts of my mind,
    be pleasing to You,
    LORD, my Rock and my Redeemer!

---

* Connecting *nizhar* with *zohar*, meaning brightness. Others 'is warned'.

PSALM 20

PRAYER FOR VICTORY

1.   For the Chief Musician. A psalm of David.

2.   May the LORD answer you in time of trouble;
      may the name of Jacob's God be a tower of strength to you.

3.   May He send you help from the sanctuary,
      and give you support from Zion.

4.   May He remember all your offerings,
      and graciously accept your burnt-offerings.   *Selah*

5.   May He grant you your heart's desire,
      and fulfil your every plan.

6.   May we shout for joy over your victory,
      and in the name of our God unfurl our banners.
      May the LORD fulfil your every wish.

7.   Now I know that the LORD will give victory to His anointed;
      He will answer him from His holy heaven
      with the saving strength of His right hand.

8.   Some boast of chariots, some of horses,
      but we boast in the name of the LORD our God.

9.   They collapse and fall,
      but we rise up and stand firm.

10.   LORD, grant victory;
      may the King answer us when we call.

PSALM 21

THANKSGIVING FOR VICTORY

1.   For the Chief Musician. A psalm of David.

2.   LORD, the king rejoices in Your might.
How great is his joy in Your saving power!

3.   For You have given him his heart's desire,
and have not denied him the request of his lips.   *Selah*

4.   You welcomed him with rich blessings,
and placed a crown of fine gold on his head.

5.   He asked You for life and You gave it to him,
length of days, for ever and ever.

6.   Great is his glory through Your victory;
You bestowed on him majesty and honour.

7.   You have given him blessings for ever,
You make him glad with the joy of Your presence.

8.   For the king trusts in the LORD,
and through the constant love of the Most High
he will not be shaken.

9.   Your hand will reach all Your enemies,
Your right hand will reach all who hate You.

10.   You will burn them up as in a fiery furnace
in the time of Your anger.
The LORD will destroy them in His anger,
fire shall consume them.

11.   You will wipe out their offspring from the earth,
and their posterity from among men.

12.   For they planned evil against You,
and devised wicked schemes,
but could not succeed.

13.   For You will make them turn their backs in flight
when You aim at their faces with Your bows.

14.   Be exalted, LORD, in Your might;
we will sing and praise Your power.

PSALM 22

THE SUFFERINGS AND HOPES OF THE VIRTUOUS MAN

1.   For the Chief Musician; *on ayyeleth ha-shahar.* A psalm of David.

2.   My God, my God, why have You forsaken me?
Why are You so far from saving me,
so far from heeding my groans?

3.   My God, I cry by day, but You do not answer;
and by night I am not silent.*

4.   Yet You are enthroned as the Holy One,
receiving the praises of Israel.

5.   In You our fathers put their trust;
they trusted, and You delivered them.

6.   They cried to You and were saved;
they trusted in You, and were not disappointed.

7.   But I am a worm, not a man,
scorned by men, despised by the people.

8.   All who see me jeer at me,
they curl their lips and wag their heads:

9.   "Let him commit himself to the LORD,
let Him save him,
let Him deliver him,
since He delights in him."

10.   But it was You who drew me from my mother's womb,
You made me secure at my mother's breast.

11.   From birth I was committed to Your charge;
from my mother's womb You have been my God.

12.   Keep not far from me,
for trouble is near, and there is no one to help.

---

*   Or 'I have no respite.'

13. Many bulls surround me,
    strong bulls of Bashan encircle me.
14. They open wide their jaws against me
    like ravenous, roaring lions.
15. I am poured out like water,
    all my bones are out of joint;
    my heart is like wax,
    it melts within me.
16. My strength is dried up like a potsherd,
    my tongue sticks to my palate;
    You lay me in the dust of death.
17. For dogs surround me,
    a mob of evil-doers encircles me,
    like a lion [they mangle] my hands and feet.
18. I can count all my bones;
    people stare and gloat over me.
19. They divide my clothing among them,
    and cast lots for my garments.

20. But You, LORD, be not far off;
    my strength, come quickly to my aid.
21. Save my life from the sword,
    my precious soul from those dogs.
22. Rescue me from the lion's jaws,
    deliver me from the horns of the wild ox.
23. Then I will declare Your fame to my brethren;
    I will praise You in the midst of the assembly.
24. Praise Him, you who fear the LORD!
    Honour Him, all you descendants of Jacob!
    Stand in awe of Him, all you descendants of Israel!
25. For He has not spurned or disdained
    the misery of the afflicted.
    He has not hidden His face from him,
    but has listened to him when he cried for help.
26. You are the theme of my praise in the great assembly;
    I will pay my vows in the presence of those who revere Him.
27. The poor shall eat and be satisfied,
    those who seek the LORD shall praise Him;
    may you be of good heart forever!

28. Let all the ends of the earth remember and turn to the LORD;
    let all the families of the nations bow down before You;
29. for dominion belongs to the LORD
    and He rules over the nations.
30. All the prosperous ones in the land shall feast
    and worship Him,
    all who are mortal* shall kneel before Him,
    even he that cannot keep his soul alive.
31. Posterity shall serve Him,
    the coming generation shall be told about the LORD;
32. and they in turn shall proclaim His righteousness
    to a people yet unborn,
    that He has acted.

---

*   Lit. 'all who go down to the dust'.

PSALM 23

THE GOOD SHEPHERD

1.   A psalm of David.

        The LORD is my shepherd; I shall not want.
2.   He makes me lie down in green pastures;
        He leads me beside still waters.
3.   He revives my soul;
        He guides me in the right paths for His name's sake.
4.   Though I walk through the valley of the shadow of death
        I fear no harm, for You are with me;
        Your rod and Your staff, they comfort me.
5.   You spread a table for me in the sight of my enemies;
        You anoint my head with oil,
        my cup overflows.
6.   Surely goodness and kindness will follow me
        all the days of my life;
        and I shall dwell in the house of the LORD
        for many years to come.

PSALM 24

THE LORD'S SOLEMN ENTRY INTO THE TEMPLE

1.   Of David. A psalm.

       The earth is the LORD's, and all that is in it;
       the world and all who live in it.
2.   For He founded it upon the seas,
       and set it firm upon the ocean currents.

3.   Who may ascend the mountain of the LORD?
       Who may stand in His holy place?
4.   He who has clean hands and a pure heart,
       who has not taken My name* in vain,
       and has not sworn deceitfully.
5.   He shall receive a blessing from the LORD,
       and generous reward from God his saviour.
6.   Such is the generation of those who seek Him;
       they are the sons of Jacob who seek Your presence. *Selah*

7.   Lift up your heads, you gates,
       lift yourselves up, you everlasting doors,
       that the King of Glory may come in.
8.   Who is the King of Glory?
       The LORD, strong and mighty,
       the LORD, mighty in battle.
9.   Lift up your heads, you gates,
       lift them up, you everlasting doors,
       that the King of Glory may come in.
10.   Who is He, this King of Glory?
       The LORD of Hosts, He is the King of Glory.   *Selah*

---

*   This rendering is based upon the traditional reading *nafshi*, 'My soul.'
Soul is often used as the equivalent of 'Name', thus paralleling the
prohibition of the third commandment not to take the name of the LORD
in vain.

PSALM 25

PRAYER FOR GUIDANCE AND PROTECTION

1.   Of David.

      To You, LORD, I lift up my soul.

2.   My God, in You I trust;
      do not let me be put to shame,
      do not let my enemies triumph over me.

3.   No one whose hope is in You is ever put to shame;
      only those are put to shame
      who wantonly break faith.

4.   Show me Your ways, LORD;
      teach me Your paths.

5.   Guide me in Your truth and teach me,
      for You are the God who will save me,
      and my hope is in You all day long.

6.   Remember, LORD, Your tender mercy and Your
      loving-kindness,
      for they are from of old.

7.   Do not remember the sins of my youth and my faults,
      but remember me according to Your love,
      in keeping with Your goodness, LORD.

8.   Good and upright is the LORD,
      therefore He instructs sinners the way they should go.

9.   He guides the humble in the right path,
      and teaches the humble His way.

10.   All the ways of the LORD are kindness and truth
      to those who keep His Covenant and His rules.

11.   For the sake of Your name, LORD,
      forgive my iniquity, though it is great.

12.   Who, then, is the man who fears the LORD?
      him will He show the path he should choose.

13.   Such a man shall live in prosperity,
           and his children shall inherit the land.

14.   The LORD confides in those who fear Him;
           to them He makes known His Covenant.

15.   My eyes are ever on the LORD,
           for only He can free my feet from the net.

16.   Turn to me and show me favour,
           for I am lonely and afflicted.

17.   The troubles of my heart have increased;
           lead me out of my distress.

18.   Look upon my affliction and my misery,
           and forgive all my sins.

19.   See how numerous are my enemies,
           how violently they hate me.

20.   Guard me and deliver me;
           let me not be put to shame,
           for I seek refuge in You.

21.   May integrity and uprightness protect me,
           for in You, LORD, is my hope.

22.   O God, redeem Israel from all its troubles.

PSALM 26

PRAYER OF THE BLAMELESS

1.   Of David.

      Vindicate me, LORD, for I have led a blameless life;
      I have trusted in the LORD;
      I have not wavered.
2.   Test me, LORD, and try me,
      probe my heart and mind.
3.   For Your love is ever before my eyes;
      I walk continually in Your truth.
4.   I do not sit in the company of false men,
      or associate with hypocrites.
5.   I detest the company of evil-doers,
      and refuse to sit with the wicked.
6.   I wash my hands in innocence,
      and join the procession round Your altar,
7.   singing songs of thanksgiving,
      and telling all Your wondrous deeds.
8.   LORD, I love the house where You dwell,
      the place where Your glory resides.
9.   Do not sweep my soul away with sinners,
      nor my life with bloodthirsty men,
10.   in whose hands are evil schemes,
      and whose right hand is full of bribes.
11.   As for me, I lead a blameless life;
      redeem me, and be merciful to me.
12.   My foot stands on level ground;
      in the assemblies I will bless the LORD.

PSALM 27

HYMN OF CONFIDENCE AND TRUST IN GOD

1.   Of David.

    The LORD is my light and my salvation;
    whom shall I fear?
    The LORD is the stronghold of my life;
    of whom shall I be afraid?

2.   When evil-doers close in on me to devour my flesh –
    it is they, my adversaries and my foes, who stumble and fall.

3.   If an army should encamp against me,
    my heart would not fear;
    if war should break out against me,
    I would still be confident.

4.   One thing I ask of the LORD, this only I seek:
    to live in the house of the LORD all the days of my life,
    to gaze upon the beauty of the LORD,
    and to worship in His temple.

5.   For He will shelter me in His pavilion
    on the day of trouble,
    He will hide me under cover of His tent,
    He will set me high upon a rock.

6.   Now my head is raised high above my enemies around me;
    I will sacrifice in His tent with shouts of joy,
    I will sing and chant praises to the LORD.

7.   LORD, hear my voice when I call;
    be gracious to me, and answer me.

8.   On Your behalf my heart says, "Seek My face!"
    Therefore I will seek Your face, LORD.

9.   Do not hide Your face from me;
    do not turn Your servant away in anger.
    You have always been my help.
    Do not reject me nor forsake me, God, my saviour.

10. Though my father and mother forsake me,
    the LORD will take me in.
11. Teach me Your way, LORD,
    and lead me on a level path,
    because of my foes who threaten me.
12. Do not hand me over to the will of my adversaries;
    for false witnesses have risen up against me,
    breathing out violence.
13. Had I not believed that I would see the LORD's goodness
    in the land of the living ...*
14. Rest your hope in the LORD, be strong and of good courage;
    and rest your hope in the LORD!

---

* The verse is left unfinished for effect; the concluding thought being 'I would have despaired.'

PSALM 28

A PLEA FOR HELP

1.   Of David.

       To You, LORD, I call;
       O my Rock, be not deaf to my cry.
       For if You remain silent,
       I shall be like those who go down to the grave.

2.   Hear my cry when I call to You for help,
       when I lift my hands towards Your holy sanctuary.

3.   Do not drag me away with the wicked,
       with evil-doers, who speak peace with their neighbours
       while malice is in their hearts.

4.   Repay them for their deeds and their malicious acts;
       repay them for what their hands have done;
       give them their deserts.

5.   For they give no thought to the works of the LORD,
       and what His hands have done;
       may He tear them down and never build them up!

6.   Blessed be the LORD
       for He has heard my cry for mercy.

7.   The LORD is my strength and my shield;
       in Him my heart trusts, and I am helped.
       Now my heart exults,
       and I praise Him with my song.

8.   The LORD is the strength of those* [loyal to Him],
       a safe refuge for His anointed.

9.   O save Your people, bless Your heritage;
       feed them and sustain them for ever!

---

*   Or: 'His people'.

PSALM 29

GOD'S MAJESTY IN THE STORM

1.   A psalm of David.

    Ascribe to the LORD, you divine beings,
    ascribe to the LORD glory and strength.

2.   Ascribe to the LORD the glory due to His name,
    worship Him in the splendour of holiness.

3.   The voice of the LORD echoes over the waters;
    the God of glory, the LORD, thunders over the mighty waters.

4.   The voice of the LORD is full of power;
    the voice of the LORD is full of majesty.

5.   The voice of the LORD breaks cedars,
    the LORD shatters the cedars of Lebanon.

6.   He makes Lebanon skip like a calf,
    Sirion like a young wild ox.

7.   The voice of the LORD flashes flames of fire.

8.   The voice of the LORD makes the desert quake;
    the LORD makes the wilderness of Kadesh tremble.

9.   The voice of the LORD makes hinds calve,
    and strips the forests bare;
    while in His temple all cry: "Glory!"

10.   The LORD was enthroned at the flood;
    the LORD sits enthroned as King for ever.

11.   The LORD will give strength to His people;
    the LORD will bless His people with peace.

PSALM 30

THANKSGIVING FOR DELIVERANCE FROM DEATH

1.   A psalm. A song for the dedication of the Temple. Of David.

2.   I will extol You, LORD,
for You have lifted me up,
and have not let my enemies rejoice over me.

3.   LORD, my God, I cried out to You,
and You healed me.

4.   LORD, You brought up my soul from Sheol,
You saved my life from going down to the pit.

5.   Sing to the LORD, O you His faithful ones,
and praise His holy name.

6.   For His anger lasts but a moment,
His favour a lifetime;
weeping may linger at nightfall,
but joy comes in the morning.

7.   When I was carefree, I thought,
"I shall never be shaken."

8.   LORD, when I enjoyed Your favour,
You made me stand firm as a mighty mountain;
when You hid Your face,
I was terrified.

9.   To You, LORD, I called;
to the LORD I pleaded:

10.   "What profit is there in my death,*
in my going down into the pit?
Can the dust acknowledge You?
Can it proclaim Your truth?"

11.   Hear, LORD, and be gracious to me;
LORD, be my helper.

---

*   Lit. 'blood'.

12.   You turned my lament into dancing;
       You removed my sackcloth and girded me with joy,
13.   that my soul may sing Your praises and never cease.
       I will acknowledge You for ever, LORD my God.

PSALM 31

A PRAYER IN TIME OF NEED

1.   For the Chief Musician. A psalm of David.

2.   In You, LORD, I take refuge,
      may I never be put to shame;
      in Your righteousness rescue me.
3.   Incline Your ear to me;
      speedily deliver me.
      Be a rock of refuge for me,
      a stronghold to save me.
4.   For You are my rock and my fortress;
      for the honour of Your name lead me and guide me.
5.   Free me from the net they have hidden for me,
      for You are my refuge.
6.   Into Your hand I commit my spirit;
      redeem me, LORD, You God of truth.
7.   I detest those who look to worthless vanities;
      for my part I put my trust in the LORD.
8.   I will exult and rejoice in Your constant love,
      for You have seen my affliction.
      You know the distress of my soul,
9.   and You have not handed me over to the enemy,
      but have set my feet at large.

10.   Have mercy on me, LORD,
      for I am in distress;
      my eye wastes away with sorrow,
      my body and soul too.
11.   My life is spent with grief,
      and my years with groaning;
      my strength fails because of my iniquity,
      and my bones waste away.

12. Because of all my foes I have become an object of scorn,
    especially so to my neighbours;
    I am a horror to my friends;
    those who see me in the street flee from me.
13. I have passed out of mind like the dead,
    I have become like a discarded vessel.
14. For I hear the whispering of many;
    there is terror on every side,
    as they conspire against me
    and plot to take my life.

15. But I trust in You, LORD;
    I say, "You are my God."
16. My fate* lies in Your hand;
    rescue me from my enemies and my pursuers.
17. Let Your face shine upon Your servant;
    save me in Your constant love.
18. LORD, let me not be put to shame when I call You;
    let the wicked be ashamed and reduced to silence in Sheol.
19. Let lying lips be struck dumb
    that speak haughtily against the righteous
    with arrogance and contempt.
20. How great is the goodness
    that You have stored up for those who fear You,
    that You have bestowed on those who take refuge in You
    in the sight of men.
21. You hide them in the shelter of Your presence
    from the intrigues of men;
    You shield them in Your tent
    from quarrelsome tongues.

22. Blessed be the LORD,
    for He has shown to me His wonderful kindness
    in a besieged city.

---

* Lit. 'my times'.

23.   In my alarm, I said,
        "I am thrust out from Your sight;"
        yet You heard my cry for mercy
        when I called to You for help.

24.   Love the LORD, all you loyal to Him!
        The LORD protects the faithful,
        but repays in full him who acts with pride.

25.   Be strong, and let your heart take courage,
        all you who wait for the LORD.

PSALM 32

THE JOY OF CONFESSION AND FORGIVENESS

1.   Of David. A *maskil*.

    Happy is he whose transgression is forgiven,
    whose sin is covered up.

2.   Happy is the man to whom the LORD imputes no guilt,
    and in whose spirit there is no deceit.

3.   All the time I suffered in silence, my body wasted away
    through my groaning all day long.

4.   For day and night Your hand lay heavy upon me;
    the sap in me dried up as by the summer's heat.   *Selah*

5.   Then I acknowledged my sin to You,
    I did not cover up my guilt.
    I said, "I will confess my transgressions to the LORD;"
    and You forgave the guilt of my sin.   *Selah*

6.   Therefore let every faithful man pray to You
    at the time when You may be found;[*]
    so that when a great flood of water comes rushing in
    it will not reach him.

7.   You are my shelter,
    You will shield me from distress;
    You will surround me with songs of deliverance.   *Selah*

8.   I will instruct you and show you
    the way you should go;
    I will counsel you, and keep My eye on you.

9.   Do not be like the horse or the mule, senseless creatures,
    whose spirit must be curbed by bit and bridle,
    so that they do not come near to you.^{**}

---

[*]   Others: 'on discovering [his sin]'.

[**]   Others: 'Or they will not come near to you.'

10. Many are the torments of the wicked,
    but love surrounds him who trusts in the LORD.
11. Rejoice in the LORD and be glad, you righteous;
    sing aloud, all you upright of heart.

PSALM 33

PRAISE OF GOD'S POWER AND PROVIDENCE

1. Sing joyfully to the LORD, you righteous;
   it is fitting for the upright to praise Him.
2. Praise the LORD with the harp;
   sing to Him with the ten-stringed lute.
3. Sing to Him a new song;
   play skilfully amid shouts of joy.
4. For the word of the LORD is right;
   His every deed is trustworthy.
5. He loves righteousness and justice;
   the earth is full of the goodness of the LORD.
6. By the word of the LORD the heavens were made,
   and all their host by the breath of His mouth.
7. He gathers the waters of the sea as in a heap;
   He puts the deep in storehouses.
8. Let all the earth fear the LORD;
   let all the inhabitants of the world stand in awe of Him.
9. For He spoke, and it was;
   He commanded, and there it stood.
10. The LORD frustrates the plans of nations;
    He thwarts the designs of peoples.
11. But the LORD's own plan stands for ever,
    the designs of His heart endure for all generations.
12. Happy is the nation whose God is the LORD;
    the people He has chosen for His own heritage.
13. The LORD looks down from heaven,
    He sees all mankind.
14. From His dwelling-place He surveys
    all the inhabitants of the earth.
15. It is He who fashions the hearts of them all,
    He notes all their doings.

16. No king is saved by the size of his army;
    no warrior is delivered by his great strength.

17.	The horse is a vain hope for deliverance;
	despite its great strength, it provides no escape.
18.	But the eye of the LORD is on those who fear Him,
	who wait for His loving care,
19.	to deliver them from death,
	and to keep them alive in famine.
20.	Our soul waits for the LORD;
	He is our help and our shield.
21.	In Him our hearts rejoice,
	for we trust in His holy name.
22.	Let Your loving care, LORD, rest upon us,
	as we have put our hope in You.

PSALM 34

PRAISE OF GOD'S CARE FOR HIS SERVANTS

1. Of David, when he feigned madness before Abimelech and was driven away, and he departed.[*]

2. I will bless the LORD at all times;
    His praise is ever in my mouth.
3. My soul glories in the LORD;
    let the humble hear it and rejoice.
4. Glorify the LORD with me;
    together let us exalt His name.
5. I sought the LORD and He answered me;
    He delivered me from all my terrors.
6. Men look to Him and are radiant;
    their faces never blush with shame.
7. This poor man cried out, and the LORD heard him;
    He saved him from all his troubles.
8. The angel of the LORD camps round those who fear Him,
    and rescues them.
9. Taste and see how good the LORD is;
    happy the man who finds refuge in Him.
10. Fear the LORD, you His holy people,
    for those who fear Him lack nothing.
11. Young lions may suffer want and go hungry,
    but those who seek the LORD lack no good thing.
12. Come, children, listen to me;
    I will teach you the fear of the LORD.
13. Who is the man who desires life,
    and longs for many days to enjoy prosperity?
14. Then keep your tongue from evil,
    and your lips from uttering deceit.
15. Shun evil and do good;
    seek peace and pursue it.

---

[*]   See 1 Sam. 21:12-16.

16.   The eyes of the LORD are on the righteous;
               His ears are open to their cry.
17.   The LORD's face is set against evil-doers,
               to cut off all memory of them from the earth.
18.   When they [the righteous] cry for help the LORD hears,
               and delivers them from all their troubles.
19.   The LORD is close to the broken-hearted;
               He saves those who are crushed in spirit.
20.   Many evils may confront the righteous man,
               but the LORD delivers him from them all.
21.   He guards every bone of his body,
               not one of them is broken.
22.   Evil brings death to the wicked;
               those who hate the righteous will suffer.
23.   The LORD redeems the lives of His servants;
               all who take refuge in Him shall never suffer.

PSALM 35

A PRAYER FOR VENGEANCE

1. Of David.

    Strive, LORD, with those who strive against me,
    fight those who fight against me.

2. Take up shield and buckler,
    and come to my defence.

3. Uncover the spear, and bar the way*
    in the face of my pursuers;
    say to me: "I am your salvation."

4. May those who seek my life be disgraced and shamed;
    may those who plot my ruin be turned back in disgrace.

5. May they be like chaff before the wind,
    with the angel of the LORD driving them on.

6. May their path be dark and slippery,
    with the angel of the LORD pursuing them.

7. For without cause they have laid their net for me;
    without cause they have dug a pit for me.

8. But destruction will overtake them unawares,
    and the net they laid will catch them;
    they will fall into it to their destruction.

9. Then my soul will rejoice in the LORD,
    and delight in His deliverance.

10. All my bones will say,
    "LORD, who is like You?
    You save the poor from one stronger than he,
    the poor and the needy from his despoiler."

11. Malicious witnesses come forward,
    they question me on things of which I know nothing.

---

*   So the Jewish commentators Rashi and Ibn Ezra. Others take the
    Hebrew word *segor* as signifying an implement of war, the battleaxe.

12. They repay me evil for good;
    [they seek] my undoing.*

13. Yet when they were sick I put on sackcloth,
    I afflicted myself with fasting.
    May it come to me what I prayed for them!

14. I went about as [though grieving] for a friend or a brother,
    bowed in gloom as though mourning for a mother.

15. But when I stumble they gather round with glee;
    even cripples gather against me;
    and those I do not know tear me to pieces without ceasing.

16. With profane mocking gestures
    they gnash their teeth at me.

17. How long, LORD, will You look on?
    Rescue my life from their onslaughts,
    my precious soul from the lions.

18. Then I will praise You in the great assembly,
    extol You before a mighty throng.

19. Let not my treacherous enemies rejoice over me;
    let not those who hate me without cause wink maliciously.

20. For they do not speak of peace,
    but devise deceitful schemes against the oppressed in the
    land.

21. They open wide their mouths against me,
    crying: "Hurrah! Hurrah! Our eye has seen it."

22. You have seen it all, LORD; be not silent.
    Do not be far from me, LORD.

23. Awake, and rise to my defence,
    to plead my cause, my God and LORD.

24. Do me justice as You are just Yourself, LORD my God;
    do not let them gloat over me.

25. Do not let them say to themselves,
    "Hurrah!, that's what we wished!"
    Let them not say, "We have swallowed him up."

---

* Lit. 'my bereavement;' alternatively 'I am all forlorn.'

26.   May those who gloat over my misfortune
       be shamed and disgraced;
       may those who exalt themselves over me
       be covered with shame and confusion.
27.   But may those who would see me vindicated
       shout for joy and gladness;
       may they always say,
       "Magnified be the LORD,
       who delights in the success of His servant!"
28.   Then shall my tongue speak of Your justice,
       and all day long of Your praise.

PSALM 36

THE GOODNESS OF GOD AND THE WICKEDNESS OF MAN

1.   For the Chief Musician. Of David, the servant of the LORD.

2.   I do believe* that sin inspires the wicked man.
There is no fear of God before his eyes.

3.   For he flatters himself in his own mind,
thinking, none can find out or hate his sin.**

4.   The words of his mouth are mischievous and deceitful;
he has given up acting sensibly or doing good.

5.   In bed he plots mischief;
he sets himself on a wicked course,
he does not reject evil.

6.   LORD, Your love reaches to heaven,
Your faithfulness to the skies.

7.   Your righteousness is like the high mountains,
Your judgements like the great deep.
LORD, You give protection to man and beast.

8.   How precious is Your love, God!
Men find refuge in the shadow of Your wings.

9,   They feast on the rich abundance of Your house;
You give them to drink of the stream of Your delights.

10.   For with You is the fountain of life;
by Your light do we see light.

11.   Continue Your love to those who know You,
and Your kindness to the upright in heart.

12.   Let not the proud foot approach me,
let not the wicked hand drive me away.

13.   There the evil doers lie fallen,
thrust down, unable to rise.

---

*   Lit. 'It is in my heart;' i.e. It is my belief.

**   i.e. 'The wicked man deceives himself that God will neither find out nor punish his sin.'

PSALM 37

THE FATE OF THE WICKED AND
THE REWARD OF THE GOOD

1.   Of David.

Do not fret because of evil-doers,
nor envy wrong-doers;

2.   for like grass they soon wither,
and like the green herbs they fade away;

3.   Trust in the LORD and do good,
settle in the land and cherish faithfulness.*

4.   Take delight in the LORD,
and He will grant you your heart's desire.

5.   Commit your way to the LORD;
trust in Him and He will act.

6.   He will make your righteousness shine like the light,
and the justice of your cause like the brightness of noon.

7.   Be patient and wait for the LORD;
do not fret over the man who prospers in his dealings,
when he carries out his evil schemes.

8.   Desist from anger and forsake wrath;
do not fret; it can only bring harm.

9.   For evil men will be cut off,
while they who hope in the LORD will inherit the land.

10.   A little longer, and the wicked will be no more;
search his place well, and he will not be there.

11.   But the humble shall inherit the land;
and enjoy abundant prosperity.

12.   The wicked man plots against the righteous
and gnashes his teeth at him;

13.   but the LORD laughs at him,
for He knows that his day will come.

---

*   Lit. 'feed on.'

14.   The wicked draw their swords and bend their bows
       to lay low the poor and the needy,
       to slaughter those who walk the straight path.
15.   Their swords shall pierce their own hearts,
       and their bows shall be broken.
16.   Better is the little which the righteous man has
       than the great wealth of the wicked;
17.   for the power of the wicked shall be broken,
       but the LORD supports the righteous.
18.   The LORD cares for the lives* of the blameless,
       and their inheritance will last for ever.
19.   They will not suffer shame in bad times;
       in days of famine they shall have plenty.
20.   But the wicked will perish;
       the enemies of the LORD will vanish
       like the beauty of the meadows;
       they shall vanish like smoke.
21.   The wicked man borrows and does not repay;
       the righteous is generous and gives again.
22.   Those blessed by Him will inherit the land,
       but those cursed by Him will be cut off.
23.   The steps of a man are made steady by the LORD,
       when He delights in the path that he takes.
24.   Though he stumbles, he will not fall headlong,
       for the LORD holds him by the hand.
25.   I have been young and now am grown old,
       yet I have never seen the righteous man forsaken,
       nor his children begging bread.
26.   At all times he is generous and lends freely,
       and his children become a blessing.
27.   Shun evil and do good,
       and you shall always live at peace.
28.   For the LORD loves justice,
       and does not forsake His faithful.
       They are safeguarded for ever;
       but the children of the wicked will be cut off.

---

*   Lit. 'days'.

29. The righteous will inherit the land,
    and dwell in it for ever.
30. The mouth of the righteous man utters wisdom,
    and his tongue speaks what is right.
31. The law of his God is in his heart;
    his footsteps will never falter.
32. The wicked watches out for the righteous,
    seeking to bring about his death;
33. but the LORD will not leave him in his power,
    nor let him be condemned when he is on trial.
34. Wait for the LORD and keep His way,
    and He will raise you to possess the land.
    When the wicked are cut off, you will see it.
35. I have seen a wicked and ruthless man,
    well-rooted like a luxurious tree in its native soil;
36. but he soon passed away and was no more;
    I sought him, but he was not to be found.

37. Watch the blameless, observe the upright,
    for there is a future for the peace-loving man.
38. But transgressors shall be utterly destroyed;
    the future of the wicked shall be cut off.
39. The deliverance of the righteous comes from the LORD;
    He is their stronghold in time of trouble.
40. The LORD helps them and delivers them;
    He delivers them from the wicked and saves them,
    because they seek refuge in Him.

PSALM 38

THE PRAYER OF ONE IN GREAT TROUBLE

1. A psalm of David. *Lehazkir.*

2. LORD, do not rebuke me in Your anger,
    or chastise me in Your wrath.
3. For Your arrows have sunk deep into me,
    and Your hand has come down upon me.
4. There is no soundness in my body
    because of Your indignation;
    there is no health in my limbs
    because of my sin.
5. For my iniquities overwhelm me,
    like a heavy load they are too heavy for me to bear.
6. My wounds stink and fester
    because of my folly.
7. I am bent double, I am utterly bowed down;
    all day long I go about in deep gloom.
8. For my loins are full of fever;
    there is no soundness in my body.
9. I am benumbed and badly crushed;
    I groan in anguish of heart.

10. LORD, all my longing lies open before You;
    my groaning is not hidden from You.
11. My heart is throbbing, my strength fails me;
    even the light has gone from my eyes.
12. My friends and my companions stand back from my
    affliction; my kinsmen stand far away.
13. Those who seek my life lay snares,
    those who mean to harm me talk of my ruin;
    they plot treachery all day long.
14. But I am like a deaf man who cannot hear,
    like a dumb man who cannot speak up.

15.   I behave like one who does not hear,
      whose mouth offers no retort.
16.   But I wait for You, LORD;
      You will answer, LORD my God.
17.   For I said,
      "Let them not rejoice over me;
      let them not gloat over me when my foot slips."
18.   For I am on the verge of disaster;[*]
      my pain is always with me.
19.   For I confess my iniquity;
      I am troubled because of my sin.
20.   My enemies are vigorous and strong;
      numerous are those who hate me without reason.
21.   Those who repay good with evil,
      oppose me for pursuing good.

22.   LORD, do not forsake me;
      my God, be not far from me.
23.   Hasten to my aid, LORD, my Deliverer.

---

[*]   Lit. 'For I am ready to fall'.

PSALM 39

A SUFFERER IN HIS DISTRESS PLEADS WITH GOD

1.   For the Chief Musician. For *Jeduthun.* A psalm of David.

2.   I said, I will watch my ways,
   lest I sin with my tongue;
   I will put a curb on my mouth,
   while the wicked man stands before me.

3.   I kept utterly silent; not a word did I say,
   not even anything good;*
   but my pain only grew worse.

4.   My heart burned within me;
   the more I thought of it, the fire flared up;
   then I spoke out without restraint:**

5.   "LORD, let me know my end
   and what is the number of my days;
   tell me how short my life is to be."

6.   Look, You have made my life but a few handbreadths;
   my life-span is as nothing before You.
   Alas, every man, however firm he stands,
   is but a mere breath.   *Selah*

7.   Alas, every man walks about as a shadow;
   alas, in vain is his restless bustle;
   he piles up wealth, not knowing who will get it.

8.   And now, what can I expect, LORD?
   My hope lies only in You.

9.   Deliver me from all my transgressions;
   do not make me the scorn of fools.

10.   I am dumb; I shall not open my mouth;
   for this is all Your doing.

---

*   So Ibn Ezra.

**   Lit. 'with my tongue'.

11. Remove Your scourge from me;
I waste away from Your blows.
12. When with rebukes You punish a man for his sin,
You make all that he treasures melt away like a moth.
Alas, man is no more than a breath. *Selah*
13. Hear my prayer, LORD; listen to my cry;
do not disregard my tears.
For I am a wayfarer before you,
a sojourner, as all my fathers were.
14. Look away from me that I may have some respite,
before I pass away and am no more.

PSALM 40

A PRAYER FOR RELIEF FROM SICKNESS

1.   For the Chief Musician. Of David. A psalm.

2.   I waited patiently for the LORD;
   He bent down to me, and heard my cry.

3.   He lifted me out of the horrible pit,
   out of the miry mud;
   He set my feet upon a rock,
   and steadied my footsteps.

4.   He put a new song into my mouth,
   a song of praise to our God.
   Many will look and stand in awe,
   and put their trust in the LORD.

5.   Happy is the man who makes the LORD his trust,
   and does not turn to the proud
   or to followers of falsehood.

6.   My LORD God, You have done great things for us;
   Your wonders and Your plans are for our good;
   none can compare with You.
   Were I to speak and tell of them,
   they would be too many to declare.

7.   You do not desire sacrifice or meal-offering;
   You do not ask for burnt-offering or sin-offering,
   but You have given me receptive ears [to obey You].

8.   Then I said, "Here I am;
   in this scroll is written my duty [to You]."

9.   My God, my whole desire is to do Your will;
   Your teaching is in my heart.

10.   I have proclaimed [Your] righteousness in the great
   assembly; I did not seal my lips, as You know, LORD.

11.   I have not kept Your kindness hidden in my heart;
   I have always spoken of Your faithfulness and saving power;
   I have never concealed Your love and Your truth
   from the great assembly.

12.   You, LORD, will not withhold Your compassion from me;
        Your kindness and true love will always protect me.

13.   For troubles without number beset me;
        my iniquities have caught up with me;
        I can no longer see.
        They are more than the hairs of my head;
        my courage fails me.

14.   Be pleased, LORD, to save me;
        LORD, hasten to my aid.

15.   Let those who seek to take my life
        be put to shame and confusion;
        let those who desire my ruin
        be turned back and disgraced.

16.   Let those who cry "Hurrah! Hurrah!" at me
        be appalled over their shame.

17.   But let all who seek You be glad and rejoice in You;
        let those who love Your saving help always say,
        "Exalted be the LORD!"

18.   But I am poor and needy,
        may the LORD think of me;
        You are my help and my rescuer;
        my God, do not delay.

PSALM 41

THANKSGIVING AFTER SICKNESS

1. For the Chief Musician. A psalm of David.

2. Happy is he who cares for the helpless!
    The LORD will deliver him on the day of trouble.
3. The LORD will protect him, and keep him alive,
    and he will be counted happy in the land.
    You will not give him up to the will of his enemies.
4. The LORD will sustain him on his sickbed;
    You will transform [to health] every ailment that he has.

5. I pray, "LORD, have mercy on me,
    heal me, for I have sinned against You."
6. My enemies say cruel things about me:
    "When will he die and his name perish?"
7. If one comes to visit me, he speaks falsehood;
    in his heart he stores up malice;
    when he leaves, he spreads it abroad.
8. All who hate me whisper together about me,
    imagining the worst for me.
9. "A vile disease courses through his body;
    now that he is bedridden, he will never rise again."
10. Even my best friend whom I trusted,
    who ate bread with me,
    lifted his heel against me.*

11. But You, LORD, have mercy on me,
    restore me, that I may repay them.
12. Then I shall know that You delight in me,
    and that my enemy will not triumph over me.
13. You have always upheld me because of my integrity,
    and kept me in Your presence for ever.

---

*   Or: 'lies in wait for me' (Rashi.)

14. Blessed be the LORD, the God of Israel,
from eternity to eternity.
Amen and Amen!

BOOK II

PSALM 42

AN EXILE'S LONGING FOR GOD AND HIS TEMPLE

1. For the Chief Musician. A *maskil* of the sons of Korah.

2. As a deer yearns for running streams,
   so does my soul yearn for You, God.
3. My soul thirsts for God, the living God.
   O when will I go and appear before God!
4. My tears have been my food day and night,
   while men say to me all day long, "Where is your God?"
5. These things I remember as I pour out my soul:
   how I used to move with the throng,
   leading them in procession to the house of God,
   amid shouts of joy and thanksgiving,
   a truly festive throng.
6. Why are you downcast, my soul?
   Why so disturbed within me?
   Hope in God; for I will yet praise Him
   for the salvation of His presence.

7. O my God, my soul is downcast within me,
   therefore I shall remember You from the land of Jordan,
   from the Hermon range and Mount Mizar,
8. where deep calls to deep in the roar of Your cataracts,
   where all Your waves and breakers have swept over me.
9. By day the LORD bestows His loving-kindness,
   and at night a song to Him is on my lips,
   a prayer to the God of my life.
10. I will say to God my rock,
    "Why have You forgotten me?
    Why must I go about mourning,
    oppressed by the enemy?"

11. Like a stab in the heart*
     are the taunts of my foes,
     when all day long they say to me,
     "Where is your God?"
12.   Why are you downcast, O my soul?
             Why so disturbed within me?
             Hope in God, for I will yet praise Him,
             my salvation and my God.

---

*   Lit. 'like murder in my bones'.

PSALM 43

THE EXILE'S PRAYER

1. Grant me justice, God, plead my cause
against an ungodly nation;
deliver me from deceitful and evil men.

2. For You are my God, my stronghold;
why have You rejected me?
Why must I go about mourning,
oppressed by the enemy?

3. Send forth Your light and Your truth
to guide me;
let them bring me to Your holy mountain,
to the place where You dwell.

4. And I will come to the altar of God,
God who is my joy and my delight;
and I will praise You with the lyre,
God, my God.

5. Why are you downcast, my soul?
Why so disturbed within me?
Hope in God; for I will yet praise Him,
my salvation and my God.

PSALM 44

A PRAYER FOR PROTECTION

1.   For the Chief Musician. A *maskil* of the sons of Korah.

2.   God, we ourselves have heard,
        our fathers have told us,
        of the deeds You performed in their days,
        in days long ago.
3.   With Your hand You displaced nations,
        and planted our fathers in their place;
        You punished the peoples and drove them out.
4.   It was not by their sword that they won the land,
        nor did their arm bring them victory;
        but it was Your right hand and Your arm,
        and the light of Your presence,
        because You favoured them.

5.   God, You are my King;
        command victory for Jacob.
6.   Through You we gore our foes;
        by Your name we trample our aggressors.
7.   For I do not trust in my bow;
        it is not my sword that brings me victory;
8.   but You give us victory over our foes;
        You put to shame those who hate us.
9.   In God we glory all day long,
        and praise Your name for ever.
        Selah

10.   But now You have rejected and humiliated us;
        You no longer go out with our armies.
11.   You have made us retreat before the foe;
        those who hate us plunder us at will.
12.   You have given us up to be devoured like sheep,
        and scattered us among the nations.

94

13. You sold Your people for next to nothing,
    and made no profit from their sale.
14. You have made us the scorn of our neighbours,
    the mockery and contempt of those around us.
15. You have made us a byword among the nations;
    the people shake their heads [at us].
16. My disgrace confronts me all day long;
    shame covers my face,
17. at the shout of those who taunt and revile me,
    because of the enemy who is bent on revenge.

18. All this has befallen us, yet we have not forgotten You,
    nor have we been false to Your Covenant.
19. Our heart has not turned back,
    nor have our feet strayed from Your path.
20. Yet You have crushed us [and cast us] into the haunt of jackals,
    and covered us with deep darkness.
21. Had we forgotten the name of our God,
    and spread out our hands to a foreign god,
22. would not God have discovered it,
    since He knows the secrets of the heart?
23. For Your sake we face death all day long,
    we are considered as sheep for slaughter.

24. Awake! Why do You sleep, LORD?
    Rouse Yourself, do not reject us for ever.
25. Why do You hide Your face,
    and forget our misery and oppression?
26. We are brought down to the dust,
    our bodies cling to the ground.
27. Arise and help us;
    for the sake of Your love redeem us.

PSALM 45

A ROYAL MARRIAGE SONG

1.   For the Chief Musician of the sons of Korah; set to
shoshanim. A *maskil*. A love song.

2.   My heart is stirred by a noble theme,
I dedicate my poem to the king.
My tongue runs like the pen of a skilful scribe.

3.   You are fairer than all mortals,
charm flows from your lips,
for God has blessed you forever.

4.   Gird your sword upon your thigh, O mighty hero,
in glory and majesty.

5.   And in your majesty ride on triumphant
for the cause of truth, humility and justice;
and may your right hand lead you to awesome deeds.

6.   Your arrows are sharp,
they pierce the hearts of your enemies;
nations fall down at your feet.

7.   Your divine throne is eternal,
Your royal sceptre is a sceptre of justice.

8.   You love right and hate wrong;
therefore God, your God, has anointed you
with oil of gladness above your fellows.

9.   Your robes are all fragrant with myrrh and aloes and cassia;
stringed music from ivory palaces delights you.

10.   Princesses are among your noble ladies;
at your right stands the queen in gold of Ophir.

11.   Listen, daughter, and consider; hear my words:
forget your own people and your father's house;

12.   let the king desire your beauty;
for he is your lord, bow to him.

13. The people of Tyre, the richest of all peoples,
    will court your favour with gifts.
14. All glorious is the princess within the palace;
    her gown is inwrought with gold.
15. In embroidered apparel she is led to the king;
    the maidens in her train, her bridesmaids, are brought to you.
16. They are led in with gladness and joy;
    they enter the palace of the king.

17. Your sons will succeed your fathers;
    you will make them princes throughout the land.
18. I will perpetuate your name throughout all generations;
    therefore peoples shall praise you for ever and ever.

PSALM 46

GOD THE STRONGHOLD OF ISRAEL

1.   For the Chief Musician. A song of the sons of Korah. On *alamoth*.

2.   God is our refuge and strength,
always ready to help in time of trouble.

3.   Therefore we are not afraid when the earth is shaken,
when mountains tumble into the heart of the sea;

4.   when its waters roar and foam
and the mountains quake at its surging.   *Selah*

5.   There is a river whose streams bring joy to the city of God,
the holy dwelling-place of the Most High.

6.   God is within her, she will never fall;
God will help her at the break of day.

7.   Nations rage, kingdoms topple;
the earth melts when He lifts His voice.

8.   The LORD of Hosts is with us,
        the God of Jacob is our fortress.   *Selah*

9.   Come and see the works of the LORD,
the astounding things He has wrought on earth.

10.   He puts an end to wars throughout the earth,
He breaks the bow, He snaps the spear;
the shield He burns with fire.

11.   Be still and know that I am God,
exalted among the nations, exalted over the earth.

12.   The LORD of Hosts is with us,
        the God of Jacob is our fortress.   *Selah*

PSALM 47

GOD THE KING OF ALL THE NATIONS

1.   For the Chief Musician. A psalm of the sons of Korah.

2.   Clap your hands, all you peoples,
        acclaim God with shouts of joy.
3.   For the LORD, the Most High, is to be revered;
        He is the great King over all the earth.
4.   He subdues peoples under us,
        He puts nations at our feet.
5.   He chose for us our heritage;
        the pride of Jacob, whom He loved.   *Selah*

6.   God ascends His throne amid shouts of joy,
        the LORD, amid blasts of the horn.
7.   Sing praises to the LORD, sing His praise,
        sing praises to our King, sing His praise.
8.   For God is king over all the earth;
        sing praises with all your skill.
9.   God reigns over the nations,
        God is seated on His holy throne.

10.   O princes of the people, gather together,
        you people, who are faithful to the God of Abraham;
        for the guardians* of the earth belong to God,
        and He is exalted above them all.

---

*   Lit. 'the shields'.

PSALM 48

A HYMN CELEBRATING THE BEAUTY AND
INVINCIBILITY OF ZION

1.   A song. A psalm of the sons of Korah.

2.   Great is the LORD, and most worthy of praise,
        in the city of our God, on His holy mountain.
3.   Beautiful in elevation,
        the joy of the whole earth is mount Zion;
        in the recesses of the north is the city of the great King.
4.   In her palaces God is known
        as a tower of strength.
5.   See, the kings join forces,
        advancing together.
6.   They saw, and they were astounded;
        they panicked; they fled in fear.
7.   Trembling seized them there,
        like the pains of a woman in labour;
8.   like the ships of Tarshish
        when an east wind wrecks them.
9.   What we have heard, we have now seen,
        in the city of the LORD of Hosts,
        in the city of our God.
        May God establish her for ever!   *Selah*

10.   In Your temple, God,
        we reflect on Your love.
11.   Your praise, God, like Your name,
        reaches to the ends of the earth.
        Your right hand is filled with kindness.
12.   Let mount Zion rejoice;
        let the cities* of Judah be glad,
        because of Your judgements.

---

*   Lit. 'daughters'.

100

13. Walk about Zion, go all round her;
    count her towers.
14. Take note of her ramparts, view her citadels,
    that you may tell it to the next generation;
15. that this God is our God for ever;
    He will guide us for evermore.[*]

---

[*] Or: 'even to the end.'

PSALM 49

THE VANITY OF WORLDLY RICHES

1.   For the Chief Musician. A psalm of the sons of Korah.

2.   Hear this, all you peoples;
listen, all you inhabitants of the world,
3.   both high and low,
rich and poor alike.
4.   My mouth shall speak words of wisdom;
the utterance of my heart shall give you understanding.
5.   I will turn my ear to a parable,
I will expound my riddle to the music of the harp.

6.   Why should I fear in evil times
when beset by the wickedness of men
who conspire against me,
7.   men who trust in their riches
and boast of their great wealth?
8.   Alas! In no way can a man redeem himself,
or pay his ransom to God –
9.   for the ransom of a life is too costly;
he must abandon the idea forever.
10.   To think that one can live on forever
and never see the grave!
11.   Surely he sees that wise men die,
that the foolish and the senseless both perish,
leaving their wealth to others.
12.   They inwardly think that their houses will continue for ever,
their dwellings for all generations;
they even name lands after themselves.
13.   But man, despite his splendour, does not endure;
he is like the beasts that perish.

14.   Such is the fate of foolish men,
and of their followers who approve their words.   *Selah*

15. Like sheep they are destined for Sheol;
    death is their shepherd.
    The upright shall rule over them in the morning,
    while their form shall waste away in Sheol,
    far from their stately homes.
16. But God will redeem my soul from the grasp of Sheol,
    for He will take me to Himself.   *Selah*

17. Fear not when a man grows rich,
    when the wealth of his house increases;
18. for he can take nothing with him when he dies,
    his wealth will not follow after him.
19. Though in his lifetime he counted himself happy –
    men always praise you when you do well for yourself –
20. he must join the company of his ancestors,
    who will never again see the light.

21. A man who has riches, but no understanding,
    is like the beasts that perish.

PSALM 50

TRUE WORSHIP

1.   A psalm of Asaph.

God, the Lord God, speaks;
He summons the whole world from east to west.

2.   From Zion, the city perfect in beauty,
God shines forth.

3.   Our God is coming, and will not be silent;
before Him is a devouring fire,
around Him a raging storm.

4.   He summons the heavens above, and the earth,
for the trial of His people.

5.   "Gather to Me My devout people,
those who made a Covenant with Me by sacrifice."

6.   The heavens proclaim His justice,
for God Himself is the judge.   *Selah*

7.   Listen, My people, and I will speak;
Israel, I will testify against you:
I am God, your God.

8.   I do not rebuke you for your sacrifices,
nor for your burnt-offerings which are ever before Me.

9.   I have no need to take bulls from your farmstead,
or he-goats from your folds;

10.   for Mine is every beast of the forest
and the cattle on thousands of hills.

11.   I know every bird on the mountains;
everything that moves in the field belongs to Me.

12.   If I were hungry, I would not tell you,
for the world is Mine and all that it holds.

13.   Do I eat the flesh of bulls,
or drink the blood of he-goats?

14.   Offer to God a sacrifice of thanksgiving,
and pay your vows to the Most High.

15. Then call upon Me in time of trouble,
     I will rescue you, and you will honour Me.

16. But to the wicked man God says:
     "What right have you to recite My laws,
     and mouth the words of My Covenant,
17. seeing that you hate correction,
     and cast My words behind you?
18. When you see a thief you associate with him;
     you throw in your lot with adulterers.
19. You give free rein to your mouth for evil,
     and harness your tongue to deceit.
20. You sit and malign your brother,
     and slander your own mother's son.
21. All this you have done, and I said nothing,
     you thought that I was like you.
     But now I will rebuke you, and indict you to your face.
22. Consider this, you who forget God,
     lest I tear you apart and there be no one to save you.
23. He who offers a sacrifice of thanksgiving honours Me,
     and to him who sets himself on My way
     I will show the salvation of God."

PSALM 51

A PRAYER OF REPENTANCE

1.   For the Chief Musician. A psalm of David, 2. when Nathan
   the prophet came to him after he had taken Bath-sheba.*

3.   God, be merciful to me in Your loving-kindness;
   in Your great compassion blot out my transgressions.
4.   Wash me thoroughly of my iniquity,
   and cleanse me from my sin.
5.   For I know my transgressions,
   I am always aware of my sin.
6.   Against You, You only, have I sinned,
   and done what is evil in Your sight;
   so You are right when You pass sentence,
   and fair in Your judgement.
7.   Truly, I have been a sinner from birth,
   sinful from the time my mother conceived me.
8.   Surely, You desire truth in our inward selves,
   so teach me wisdom about hidden things.

9.   Purge me with hyssop and I shall be pure;
   wash me and I shall be whiter than snow.
10.   Let me hear the sound of joy and gladness;
    let the bones You have crushed rejoice.
11.   Hide Your face from my sins
    and blot out all my iniquities.
12.   Create in me a pure heart, God,
    and put a new steadfast spirit within me.
13.   Do not cast me away from Your presence,
    or take Your holy spirit away from me.
14.   Grant me once again the joy of Your saving power;
    let Your noble spirit sustain me.

---

*   See 2 Sam. 12.

15. Then I will teach transgressors Your ways,
    and sinners will return to You.

16. Deliver me from bloodshed, O God, God my Deliverer,
    and my tongue will sing of Your righteousness.

17. LORD, open my lips,
    and my mouth will declare Your praise.

18. You take no delight in sacrifice,
    or I would bring it;
    You do not desire burnt-offerings.

19. The sacrifice acceptable to God is a broken spirit;
    a wounded and contrite heart,
    You, God, will not despise.

20. May it be Your pleasure to make Zion prosper;
    rebuild the walls of Jerusalem.

21. Then You will delight in sincere offerings,
    in burnt-offerings and whole-offerings;
    then bullocks will be offered on Your altar.

PSALM 52

THE HATE OF THE DECEITFUL

1.   For the Chief Musician. A *maskil*. Of David, 2. when Doeg
   the Edomite came and told Saul that David had gone to
   Ahimelech's house.[*]

3.   Why do you boast of your wickedness, you brave man?
   God's loving-kindness is all day long.
4.   You plot ruin,
   your tongue is sharp as a razor, you mischief-maker.
5.   You love evil rather than good,
   falsehood rather than speaking the truth.   *Selah*
6.   You love the destructive word,
   the deceitful tongue.
7.   Surely God will utterly destroy you,
   He will snatch you up and pluck you from your tent,
   and uproot you out of the land of the living.   *Selah*
8.   The righteous will look on, awe-struck;
   they will gloat over him and say,
9.   "So this is the man who would not make God his refuge,
   but trusted in his great wealth,
   and grew powerful by his mischief."

10.   But I am like a flourishing olive tree in God's house;
    I trust in the goodness of God for ever and ever.
11.   I will praise You for ever for what You have done;
    I will proclaim that Your name is good
    in the presence of Your loyal ones.

---

[*]   See 1 Sam. 22:9ff.

PSALM 53

THE WICKEDNESS OF MANKIND

I.   * For the Chief Musician; on *mahalath*. A *maskil* of David.

2.   The fool says in his heart,
"There is no God."
All are corrupt, they do abominable deeds;
no one does good.

3.   God looks down from heaven on mankind
to see if there are any who act wisely,
any who seek God.

4.   But they are all dross,
all rotten to the core;
there is no one who does good,
not even one.

5.   Will the evil-doers never learn,
who devour My people as men eat bread,
and never call upon God?

6.   There they are, in dire terror;
never was there such terror.
For God has scattered the bones of your attackers.
You have put them to shame,
for God has rejected them.

7.   O that the deliverance of Israel might come from Zion!
When God restores the fortunes of His people,
Jacob will rejoice, Israel will be glad.

---

* This psalm is a revised form of Psalm 14. Here the Divine name is exclusively 'God', whereas in Psalm 14 'the LORD' is used.

PSALM 54

CRY FOR GOD'S HELP

1.   For the Chief Musician, with stringed instruments. A *maskil* of David, 2. when the Ziphites came and told Saul: "We are sure David is in hiding among us."[*]

3.   Save me, God, by Your name;
   vindicate me, by Your might.
4.   God, hear my prayer;
   give ear to the words of my mouth.
5.   For strangers have risen up against me,
   ruthless men seek my life,
   men who have no regard for God.   *Selah*

6.   But God is my helper;
   the LORD is the sustainer of my life.
7.   He will repay the evil of my foes;
   by Your faithfulness destroy them.
8.   Then I will willingly offer sacrifice to You;
   I will praise Your name, LORD, for it is good.
9.   For He has delivered me from all trouble,
   and my eyes have seen the downfall of my enemies.

---

[*]   See Sam. 23:19.

PSALM 55

DISTRESS OF A MAN BETRAYED BY HIS FRIEND

1.   For the Chief Musician; with stringed instruments. A *maskil*
     of David.

2.   Give ear, God, to my prayer;
     do not hide Yourself from my plea.
3.   Listen to me and answer me;
     I am restless in my grief, and am distraught
4.   at the clamour of the enemy,
     because of the oppression of the wicked;
     for they bring down misery upon me,
     and fiercely assail me.
5.   My heart is in anguish within me,
     the terrors of death bear down on me.
6.   Fear and trembling have beset me,
     horror overwhelms me.
7.   I said, "O that I had the wings of a dove!
     I would fly away and be at rest;
8.   I would flee far away,
     I would lodge in the wilderness.   *Selah*
9.   I would quickly find a shelter for myself
     from the raging wind and the tempest."

10. LORD, confuse and break up their schemes!*
     For I see violence and strife in the city;
11. day and night they go around its walls;
     trouble and mischief are in its midst.
12. There is destruction everywhere;
     fraud and deceit never depart from its streets.

---

*   Lit. 'their tongue.'

13. Yet, it is not an enemy who reviles me –
    that I could bear;
    nor is it a foe of mine who treats me with scorn –
    for then I could hide from him.
14. But it is you, a man like myself,
    my companion, my intimate friend;
15. we used to take sweet counsel together,
    as we walked with the throng* to the house of God.
16. May He incite death against them;
    may they go down alive into Sheol,
    for evil is in their dwellings, in their very midst.

17. But I call to God,
    and the LORD will save me.
18. Evening, morning and noon
    I complain and moan,
    and He hears my voice.
19. He rescues me unharmed from the battle
    that is waged against me;
    for many are hostile to me.
20. God, who is enthroned from of old,
    will hear and humble them.   *Selah*
    For these people never change,
    and have no fear of God.
21. That man** attacked those who were at peace with him,
    he violated his covenant of friendship.
22. His speech was smoother than butter,
    yet war was in his heart;
    his words were more soothing than oil,
    yet they were swords, drawn.

23. Cast your cares upon the LORD and He will sustain you;
    He will never let the righteous man fall.

---

*   Or: 'with ecstasy'.
**   i.e. the 'friend' of v. 14.

24.   For You, God, will bring them down into the deepest pit;
bloodthirsty and deceitful men
shall not live out half their days;
but I, for my part, will put my trust in You.

PSALM 56

TRUST IN GOD, THE HELPER IN NEED

1   For the Chief Musician; on *jonath elem rehokim*. David. A
miktam; when the Philistines seized him in Gath.

2.   Have mercy on me, God, for men trample me underfoot;
all day long assailants harass me.
3.   My foes trample on me all day long;
for many are those who assail me, O Most High.
4.   When I am afraid, I put my trust in You.
5.   In God, whose word I praise,
in God I trust, I shall not fear;
what can mortal man do to me?
6.   All day long they distort my words,*
all their thought is to harm me.
7.   They band together, they lie in wait,
they watch my steps, eager to take my life.
8.   For such crimes are they to go unpunished?**
God, in Your anger cast down such people.

9.   Do keep count of my wanderings;
store my tears in Your flask.
Surely they are recorded in Your book.
10.   Then my enemies will turn back
when I call for help;
for this I know, that God is on my side.

11.   In God, whose word I praise,
in the LORD, whose word I praise,
12.   in God I trust, I shall not fear;
what can man do to me?

---

*   Or: 'They vex me for my word'.
**   Lit. 'is deliverance for them.'

13.   I must pay the vows I made to You, God;
             I will render thank-offerings to You.
14.   For You have rescued my soul from death,
             my feet from stumbling,
             that I may walk before God in the light of life.

PSALM 57

PRAYER IN THE MIDST OF DANGER

1. For the Chief Musician; *al tashheth*. Of David. A *miktam*;
when he fled from Saul into a cave.

2. Have mercy on me, God, have mercy,
for in You does my soul take refuge.
In the shadow of Your wings I take refuge
until the storms of destruction have passed.

3. I call to God Most High,
to God who will make all end well for me.

4. He will send from heaven and save me
from the reproach of him who would trample me
down.   *Selah*
God will send His love and His faithfulness.

5. I am among lions;
I lie down among hotheads,
men whose teeth are spears and arrows,
whose tongue is a sharp sword.

6.   Be exalted, God, above the heavens;
    let Your glory be over all the earth.

7. They have spread a net for my feet,
my spirit is low;
they have dug a pit in my path,
but have themselves fallen into it.   *Selah*

8. My heart is steadfast, God,
my heart is steadfast;
I will sing and chant praises.

9. Awake, O my soul!
Awake, harp and lyre!
I will awaken the dawn.

10. I will praise You, LORD, among the nations;
I will sing praises to You among the peoples.

11.   For Your love is as high as the heavens;
           Your faithfulness reaches to the sky.
12.   Be exalted, God, above the heavens;
               let Your glory be over all the earth.

PSALM 58

AGAINST WICKED JUDGES

1.   For the Chief Musician; *al tashheth*. A psalm of David. A
miktam.

2.   You judges,* do you really dispense justice?
Do you judge people with fairness?

3.   In your heart you devise injustice;
with your hands you deal out violence in the land.

4.   The wicked are perverse from birth,
they go astray as soon as they are born, always speaking lies.

5.   Their venom is like the venom of serpents;
they are like the deaf asp which stops its ears

6.   so as not to listen to the sound of the charmer,
or to the expert caster of spells.

7.   God, break the teeth in their mouths;
LORD, shatter the fangs of these young lions.

8.   May they melt and vanish like water.
May He aim His arrows till they are cut to pieces.

9.   May they be like the snail which dissolves as it moves along,
like a stillborn child, which never sees the sun!

10.   Before your pots can feel [the heat of] the thorns,
He will whirl them away by His might and in His fury.

11.   The righteous man shall rejoice when he sees vengeance
done;
he will bathe his feet in the blood of the wicked.

12.   Then men will say:
"There is, after all, reward for the righteous;
there is, indeed, a God who does justice on earth."

---

* The Hebrew, *elem*, here translated 'judges', may be a defective spelling
for *elim*, 'gods', which term embraces judges and rulers; cf. Ex.15:11,
21:6.

PSALM 59

A PRAYER FOR DELIVERANCE FROM
WICKED ENEMIES

1   For the Chief Musician; *al tashheth*. A psalm of David. A
miktam, when Saul sent men to watch on David's house to
kill him. *

2.   Rescue me from my enemies, O my God;
be my strong tower against my assailants.

3.   Rescue me from evil-doers;
save me from bloodthirsty men.

4.   See, they lie in wait for my life;
fierce men band together against me
for no offence or sin of mine, LORD.

5.   For no guilt of mine they rush and are ready [to attack].
Rouse Yourself on my behalf; see my plight.

6.   For You, LORD God of Hosts, are the God of Israel;
bestir Yourself, and punish all the nations;
show no mercy to wicked traitors.   *Selah*

7.   They come out at nightfall, snarling like dogs,
and prowl about the city.

8.   See, they emit a stream of abuse from their mouths,
words like swords are on their lips;
[They say,] "Who can hear us?"

9.   But You, LORD, laugh at them;
You mock all the nations.

---

*   See Sam. 19:11.

10. O Mighty One!* I wait for You,
   for God is my strong tower.
11. God who shows me love will go before me;
   God will let me gloat over my foes.
12. But do not kill them, lest my people forget;
   scatter them by Your might.
   Bring them to ruin, LORD, our Shield,
13. for the sins they have uttered,
   for the words of their lips.
   Let them be taken in their pride,
   for the curses and the lies which they utter.
14. Destroy them in Your anger,
   destroy them till they are no more,
   then it will be known to the ends of the earth,
   that God is ruler in Jacob.   *Selah*

15. They come out at nightfall, snarling like dogs,
   as they prowl about the city.
16. They wander about in search of food,
   and howl if they are not satisfied.
17. But I will sing of Your strength,
   every morning I will extol Your love;
   for You have been to me a tower of strength,
   a refuge in times of trouble.

18. O my Mighty One, I will sing praise to You;
   for God is my strong tower,
   the God who shows me love.

---

* Taking the Hebrew *uzzo* (or *uzzu*) as the archaic form of the noun *oz*, meaning strength or might. The Psalmist appeals to God for help, addressing Him as the Mighty One. After receiving help from God in v.18, he addresses God as 'my Mighty One'.

PSALM 60

PRAYER AFTER DEFEAT IN BATTLE

1. For the Chief Musician; on *shushan eduth*. A *miktam* of
    David, for instruction; 2. [*] when he fought against Aram-
    Naharaim and Aram-Zobah, while Joab returned and killed
    twelve thousand Edomites in the Valley of Salt.

3. God, You have rejected us and shattered us;
    You have been angry; restore us!
4. You have shaken the land and torn it open;
    repair its ruins, for it is falling apart.
5. You have made Your people suffer hardship;
    You have given us wine that makes us stagger.
6. But You have raised a banner for those who fear You
    round which they may rally for the sake of truth.   *Selah*
7. ^{**} That those dear to You may be delivered,
    save with Your right hand and answer me.

8. God declared in His sanctuary that I would triumph;
    I would divide Shechem,
    and measure off the Valley of Sukkoth.
9. Gilead would be mine, Manasseh mine;
    Ephraim my chief stronghold, Judah my sceptre.
10. Moab would be my washbasin,
    over Edom I would fling my shoe;
    Philistia, come and join me.

11. But who will conduct me to the fortified city?
    Who will lead me to Edom?
12. Have You not rejected us, God?
    No longer, God, do You come out with our armies.

---

[*] See Sam. 8, and 1 Chron. 18.
[**] With vv.7-14, cf. Ps.108, 7-14.

13. Grant us aid against the foe,
for worthless is the help of man.
14. Through God we shall do valiantly,
for He will trample our foes.

PSALM 61

PRAYER OF AN EXILE

1. For the Chief Musician; with a stringed instrument. A psalm
    of David.

2. God, hear my cry,
    listen to my prayer.
3. From the end of the earth I call to You
    when my heart grows faint;
    lead me to a rock that is high above me.
4. For You have been my refuge,
    a tower of strength against the foe.
5. O that I may dwell in Your tent for ever,
    and take refuge in the shelter of Your wings.   *Selah*
6. For You, God, have heard my vows;
    grant the request* of those who fear Your name.

7. Add days to the life of the king!
    May his years extend over many generations!
8. May he sit enthroned in God's presence for ever;
    appoint Your constant love to protect him!
9. So I will ever sing praises to Your name,
    as I fulfil my vows day after day.

---

*   Or: 'Restore the heritage'.

PSALM 62

GOD IS A SAFE REFUGE

1.   For the Chief Musician; on *Jeduthun*. A psalm of David.

2.   For God alone my soul waits patiently,
my deliverance comes only from Him.

3.   He alone is my rock and my deliverance;
He is my fortress; I shall never be shaken.

4.   How long will all of you assault a man
and batter him down,
as if he were a leaning wall,
a tottering fence?

5.   They plan only to topple him from his height;
they delight in lies.
With their mouths they bless,
but in their hearts they curse.   *Selah*

6.   For God alone wait patiently, O my soul;
for my hope comes only from Him.

7.   He alone is my rock and my deliverance;
He is my fortress; I shall not be shaken.

8.   Upon God depend my deliverance and honour;
He is the rock of my strength.
In God is my refuge.

9.   Trust in Him at all times, O people;
pour out your hearts before Him,
for God is our refuge.   *Selah*

10.   Men of low degree are a mere breath,
men of high degree are but an illusion;
placed on the scales all together,
they are lighter than a breath.

11.   Put not your trust in extortion,
nor place vain hope in robbery;
though your riches increase,
set not your heart on it.

12. One thing God has spoken,
two things indeed have I learnt:
13. that power belongs to God,
and that with You, LORD, is love.
And You will reward each man according to his deeds.

PSALM 63

ARDENT LONGING FOR GOD

1.	A psalm of David, when he was in the wilderness of Judah.

2.	God, You are my God; eagerly I seek You.
	My soul thirsts for You,
	my body longs for You,
	like a parched and weary land that has no water.
3.	So do I long to see You in the sanctuary,
	and to behold Your power and glory!
4.	For Your love is better than life itself;
	therefore my lips will sing Your praises.
5.	Thus I will bless You as long as I live;
	in Your name I lift up my hands [in prayer].

6.	My soul is satisfied as with the richest of foods;*
	my mouth shall praise You with joyous lips.
7.	When I lie in bed I remember You;
	through the watches of the night I think of You;
8.	for You have always been my help;
	in the shadow of Your wings I sing for joy.
9.	My soul clings to You;
	Your right hand supports me.

10.	May those who seek to destroy my life
	sink into the depths of the earth.
11.	May they be given over to the sword,
	and become the prey of foxes.
12.	But the king shall rejoice in God;
	all who swear by Him shall glory,
	while the mouths of liars will be stopped.

---

*	Lit. 'marrow and fat'.

PSALM 64

TREACHEROUS CONSPIRATORS
ARE PUNISHED BY GOD

1. For the Chief Musician; a Psalm of David.

2. Hear my voice, God, when I plead;
   guard my life from the terror of the enemy.

3. Hide me from the council of wicked men,
   from the riotous mob of evil-doers,

4. who sharpen their tongues like swords,
   and aim venomous words like arrows,

5. to shoot from ambush at the innocent,
   shooting at him suddenly, without fear.

6. They encourage each other in their evil scheme;
   they talk about laying hidden snares.
   They say, "Who can see them?"

7. They thoroughly test their plots;
   they conceal a well-devised scheme –
   deep indeed is the heart and mind of man.

8. But God shoots an arrow at them,
   suddenly they are stricken.

9. Their own tongue shall trip them up,
   all who see them shall flee in horror.

10. Then all men shall stand in awe;
    they will declare the work of God
    and understand what He has done.

11. The righteous will rejoice in the LORD,
    and take refuge in Him;
    all the upright in heart will exult.

PSALM 65

THANKSGIVING FOR GOD'S BLESSING

1.   For the Chief Musician. A psalm of David. A song.

2.   To You, God in Zion, silence is praise;
       to You vows are paid.
3.   Hearer of prayer,
       to You all men shall come.
4.   When sinfulness overwhelms me;
       only You can forgive our transgressions.
5.   Happy is he whom You choose and bring near
       to dwell in Your courts!
       May we be filled with the bounty of Your house,
       of Your holy temple!
6.   By Your righteousness answer us with wondrous deeds,
       God, our deliverer,
       in whom all the ends of the earth and the distant seas
       put their trust.
7.   It is He who by His might made the mountains firm;
       so girded with power is He.
8.   He stills the raging of the seas,
       the roaring of their waves,
       and the tumult of the peoples.
9.   Those who live at the ends of the earth
       are overawed by Your signs.
       You make the lands of sunrise and sunset sing with joyous
       song.

10.   You care for the land and water it;
       You enrich it greatly
       with God's stream that is full of water;
       and so You provide grain [for man].
       In this manner You prepare the earth:

11. You water its furrows,
    You level its ridges,
    You soften it with showers,
    You bless its growth.
12. You crown the year with Your goodness;
    Your tracks drip with abundance.
13. The desert pastures drip with moisture,
    the hills are girded with joy.
14. The meadows are clothed with sheep,
    the valleys are decked with grain;
    they shout for joy, they break into song.

PSALM 66

PRAISE OF GOD, ISRAEL'S DELIVERER

1.   For the Chief Musician. A song. A psalm.

    Shout with joy to God, all you on earth.
2.   Sing to the glory of His name;
    make glorious His praise.
3.   Say to God, "How awesome are Your deeds!"
    Because of Your mighty power
    Your enemies cower before You.
4.   All the earth bows to You
    and sings praises to You;
    they sing praises in honour of Your name.   *Selah*

5.   Come and see the works of God;
    awesome are His deeds among men.
6.   He turned the sea into dry land,
    that men may pass through the river on foot;
    therefore let us rejoice in Him.
7.   He rules for ever by His power,
    His eyes keep watch on the nations;
    let not the rebellious exalt themselves.   *Selah*

8.   Bless our God, O nations;
    let the sound of His praise be heard,
9.   for He has kept us among the living,
    and has not let our feet slip.

10. For You, God, have put us to the test,
    and refined us as one refines silver;
11. You have led us into a snare,
    and placed shackles around our loins;
12. You have let men ride over our heads;
    we went through fire and water,
    but You have led us forth to freedom.*

13. I enter Your house with burnt-offerings,
    and pay my vows to You –
14. vows which my lips pronounced,
    and my mouth uttered when I was in distress.
15. I will offer up to You fat beasts as burnt-offerings,
    and the soothing odour of burning rams;
    I will make ready bulls and he-goats.   *Selah*

16. Come and hear, all you God-fearing men,
    and I will tell you what He did for me.
17. With my mouth I called to Him,
    high praise was on my tongue.
18. Had I evil thoughts in my mind,
    the LORD would not have listened.
19. But God did listen,
    He gave heed to my prayer.
20. Blessed be God who has not turned away my prayer
    nor His loving-kindness from me.

---

* Lit. 'overflowing ease'.

PSALM 67

A PRAYER FOR GOD'S BLESSING

1.　　For the Chief Musician; with stringed instruments. A psalm.
　　　A song.

2.　　May God be gracious to us and bless us;
　　　may He cause His face to shine upon us,　　　　*Selah*
3.　　that Your way may be known on earth,
　　　Your salvation, among all nations.
4.　　May the peoples praise You, God;
　　　may all the peoples praise You!
5.　　The nations will rejoice and break into song;
　　　for You judge the peoples with equity
　　　and guide the nations of the earth.　　　　　*Selah*
6.　　May the peoples praise You, God;
　　　may all the peoples praise You!
7.　　The earth has yielded its produce;
　　　may God, our God, bless us.
8.　　May God bless us,
　　　and may all the ends of the earth fear Him!

PSALM 68

GOD'S TRIUMPHAL PROCESSION

1.   For the Chief Musician. A psalm. A song of David.

2.   May God arise, may His enemies be scattered;
    may those who hate Him flee before Him.
3.   As smoke is dispersed [by the wind], so disperse them;
    as wax melts before fire, so shall the wicked perish
    before God.
4.   But the righteous shall rejoice and exult before God;
    they shall be happy and joyful.

5.   Sing to God; sing praises to His name;
    extol Him who rides on the clouds.
    The LORD is His name; exult before Him.
6.   The father of the fatherless, the defender of the widow,
    is God in His holy dwelling.
7.   God gives the lonely a home,
    He leads out the imprisoned to prosperity;
    but the rebellious shall live in a parched land.

8.   God, when You went forth before Your people,
    when You marched through the wasteland,   *Selah*
9.   the earth trembled, the heavens poured down rain,
    at the sight of God;
    Sinai too [quaked], at the sight of God, the God of Israel.

10.   You, God, poured down a generous rain,
    and refreshed Your weary heritage.
11.   Then Your own people settled there;
    in Your goodness, God, You provided for the needy.
12.   The LORD spoke the tidings [of victory],
    a great host of women spread the news:
13.   "Kings with their armies are in flight, in flight,
    while the women at home divide the spoil."

14. Even for those of you who lay idly among the sheepfolds,
there were wings of a dove sheathed in silver,
its pinions in glittering gold.*

15. When the Almighty scattered the kings,
it was like snow falling on Mount Zalmon.

16. Mount Bashan is a lofty mountain,
Mount Bashan with its many peaks.

17. Why gaze in envy, you many-peaked mount,
at the mountain God desired for His dwelling?
The LORD will abide there for ever.

18. The chariots of God are many myriads,
thousands upon thousands;
the LORD was among them.
So it was at Sinai, so, too, as He entered the sanctuary.

19. You, God, ascended the heights, You carried off captives,
You received tributes from men, even from rebels,
that the LORD God might dwell there.

20. Blessed be the LORD who bears our burdens day by day;
God is our salvation.   *Selah*

21. Our God is a God who saves;
the LORD God can provide escape from death.

22. But God will crush the heads of His enemies,
the hairy scalp of him who persists in his guilt.

23. The LORD said, "I will bring them back from Bashan,
I will bring them back from the depths of the sea,

24. that your feet may wade through blood,
and the tongues of your dogs may have their share of the
enemy."

25. The people saw Your processions, God,
the processions of my God, my King, into the sanctuary;

26. the singers in the lead, the minstrels following,
among them maidens beating timbrels.

27. In full assemblies bless God;
[bless] the LORD, you who are from the fountain of Israel.

---

* These were the trophies taken from the enemy.

28. There was the little tribe of Benjamin leading them,
    there the princes of Judah in their brocaded robes,
    there, too, the princes of Zebulun and the princes
    of Naphtali.
29. Your God endowed you with strength [in the past];
    display again, God, that strength which You wrought for us.
30. For the honour of Your Temple at Jerusalem
    kings will bring You gifts.
31. Rebuke the wild beast of the reeds,
    the herd of bulls with the calves of the nations,
    until, humbled, they each come with pieces of silver.
    Scatter the peoples who delight in wars.
32. Envoys will come from Egypt,
    Ethiopia will stretch out her hands to God.

33. Sing to God, O kingdoms of the earth;
    Sing praises to the LORD,   *Selah*
34. to Him who rides on the heavens, the ancient heavens.
    Listen! His voice thunders with mighty power.
35. Ascribe power to God,
    whose majesty is over Israel,
    whose might is in the clouds.
36. You are awesome, God, in Your sanctuary!
    He is Israel's God who gives might and power to the people.
    Blessed be God!

PSALM 69

A PRAYER FOR GOD'S PROTECTION

1.   For the Chief Musician. On *shoshanim*. A psalm of David.

2.   Save me, God, for the waters have come up to my neck.
3.   I have sunk into the miry depths, where there is no foothold;
     I have come into deep waters,
     and the flood carries me away.
4.   I am weary with crying, my throat is dry;
     my eyes grow dim while I wait for my God.
5.   More numerous than the hairs of my head
     are those who hate me without cause;
     many are those who would destroy me,
     who are wrongfully my enemies.
     How can I restore what I have not stolen?

6.   God, You know how foolish I have been;
     my guilty deeds are not hidden from You.
7.   LORD God of Hosts, let not those who hope in You
     be put to shame because of me.
     Let not those who seek You be dismayed
     because of me, O God of Israel.
8.   It is for Your sake that I suffer reproach,
     that shame covers my face.
9.   I have become a stranger to my brothers,
     an alien to the sons of my own mother.
10.   Zeal for Your house has consumed me;
     the insults of those who revile You have fallen upon me.
11.   When I wept and fasted,
     I was taunted for it.
12.   When I put on sackcloth,
     I became a byword among them.
13.   Those who sit by the town gate talk about me;
     I am the song of drunkards.

14. But I, LORD, I pray to You –
    may it be at a favourable moment!
    In Your abundant love answer me, God,
    with the assurance of Your deliverance.

15. Rescue me from the mire; let me not sink;
    let me be rescued from my enemies,
    and from the deep waters.

16. Let not the flood waters carry me away;
    do not let the deep swallow me up,
    and let not the Pit close its mouth over me.

17. Answer me, LORD, according to Your loving-kindness;
    in Your great compassion turn to me.

18. Do not hide Your face from Your servant;
    answer me quickly for I am in great trouble.

19. Come near to me and redeem me;
    free me from my foes.

20. You know my reproach, my shame and my disgrace;
    all who harass me are well-known to You.

21. Their insults have broken my heart,
    and I am desperately sick;
    I look for sympathy, but there is none,
    for comforters, but find none.

22. They put poison in my food;
    for my thirst they gave me vinegar to drink.

23. May their table be a snare to them,
    and a trap to them in their security. *

24. May their eyes be darkened so that they cannot see;
    make their loins shake continually.

25. Pour out Your wrath upon them;
    and let Your fierce anger overtake them.

26. May their settlements be deserted,
    let there be no one to live in their tents.

27. For they persecute him whom You have struck down,
    and gossip about the pain of those whom You have wounded.

28. Charge them with crime upon crime,
    and let them not enjoy Your favour.

---

*   Or: 'and a trap to their allies'.

29. Let them be blotted out from the book of life,
and not be inscribed among the righteous.

30. But I am afflicted and in pain;
let Your help, God, raise me on high.

31. Then will I praise God's name with a song,
and exalt Him with thanksgiving.

32. This will please the LORD more than any bull,
or bullock with horns and cloven-hoof.

33. The humble will see this and rejoice;
take heart, you seekers after God.

34. For the LORD listens to the needy,
and does not despise His captive people.

35. Let heaven and earth praise Him,
the seas and all that moves in them.

36. For God will save Zion,
and rebuild the cities of Judah;
they shall live there and inherit it.

37. The descendants of His servants shall possess it,
and those who love His name shall dwell there.

PSALM 70

A CRY FOR HELP

1.   For the Chief Musician. A psalm of David; *lehazkir*.

2.   Make haste, God, to save me;
           come quickly to my aid!

3.   Ashamed and confounded be those who seek my life!
           Routed and disgraced be those who desire my ruin!

4.   May they withdraw in their shame
           who jeer, crying, "Hurrah! Hurrah!"

5.   But may all who seek You be glad and jubilant in You;
           may those who love Your saving power
           forever say, "God is great!"

6.   But I am poor and needy,
           God, come quickly to me.
           You are my help and my deliverer,
           LORD, do not tarry!

PSALM 71

PRAYER IN OLD AGE

1. In You, LORD, I take refuge;
   may I never be put to shame.
2. In Your righteousness deliver me and rescue me;
   turn Your ear to me and save me.
3. Be my stronghold, my shelter,
   to which I may come at all times;
   order* my deliverance,
   for You are my rock and my fortress.
4. Rescue me, O my God, from the power of the wicked,
   from the grasp of evil and violent men.

5. For You are my hope, LORD God,
   my trust since my childhood.
6. In the womb I was dependent on You;
   it was You who brought me forth from my mother's womb.
   I will praise You at all times.
7. I have become a source of wonder to many;
   but You are my strong refuge.
8. My mouth is full of praise to You,
   singing Your glory all day long.
9. Do not cast me off in old age,
   do not forsake me when my strength fails.
10. For my enemies talk against me,
    those who watch for my life take counsel together,
11. saying, "God has forsaken him;
    pursue him, catch him; for there is no one to save him."
12. God, be not far from me;
    my God, hasten to my help.
13. May my accusers be shamed and ruined;
    may those who seek my hurt be covered with scorn and
    disgrace!

---

* Taking the verb in the precative sense.

14. But as for me, I will always hope,
    and praise You ever more and more.
15. My mouth will tell of Your righteousness,
    all day long of Your saving acts,
    though I know not how to tell it all.
16. I come [to praise You] for Your mighty acts, LORD God;
    and I will proclaim Your righteousness, Yours alone.
17. God, You have been my teacher from my youth,
    and to this day I tell of Your marvellous deeds.
18. So now that I am old and grey-headed,
    do not forsake me, God,
    until I proclaim Your power to the next generation,
    and Your might, to all who are to come.
19. Your righteousness, God, reaches to highest heaven,
    for great are the things You have done.
    Who is there like You, God?
20. Though You have made me undergo many bitter troubles,
    yet You will revive me once more,
    and raise me once more from the depths of the earth.
21. You will increase my honour,
    and comfort me again.
22. Then I will praise You with the lyre
    for Your faithfulness, O my God.
    I will sing praises to You with the harp,
    O Holy One of Israel.
23. My lips shall greatly rejoice as I sing praises to You;
    my whole being, too, which You have redeemed.
24. All day long my tongue shall tell of Your righteousness,
    how those who sought my hurt were shamed and disgraced.

PSALM 72

THE KINGDOM OF PEACE

1.   Of Solomon.

    God, endow the king with Your justice,
    the royal son with Your righteousness,

2.   that he may judge Your people with righteousness,
    and Your poor with equity.

3.   May the mountains bring forth prosperity for the people,
    the hills too, because of [his] justice.

4.   May he defend the poor among the people;
    may he save the children of the needy,
    and crush the oppressor.

5.   Then all will revere You as long as the sun endures,
    and as long as the moon lasts, throughout the ages.

6.   May he come down
    like rain falling on a mown field,
    like showers watering the earth.

7.   In his days may the righteous flourish,
    and peace abound till the moon be no more.

8.   May he rule from sea to sea,
    from the River to the ends of the earth.

9.   Desert dwellers shall kneel before him;
    his enemies shall lick the dust.

10.   The kings of Tarshish and of the isles shall pay him tribute,
    the kings of Sheba and Seba shall offer gifts;

11.   all kings shall bow to him,
    all nations shall serve him.

12.   For he saves the needy who call for help,
    and the poor who have no protector.

13.   He has pity on the poor and the needy,
    and saves the lives of the helpless.

14.   He redeems their lives from oppression and violence,
for their blood is precious in his eyes.

15.   Long may he live!
May he be given gold from Sheba!
May prayer be made for him continually,
and blessings be his all the day long!

16.   May there be an abundance of corn in the land,
even on the mountain tops;
may its crops rustle like Lebanon;
and men shall thrive in the cities like grass in the fields.

17.   May his name endure for ever;
as long as the sun lasts may his name continue;
men shall wish to be blessed as he was;
all nations shall call him happy!

18.   Blessed be the LORD, the God of Israel,
who alone does wondrous things!

19.   Blessed be His glorious name for ever;
let the whole earth be filled with His glory!
Amen and Amen!

20.   Here end the prayers of David, son of Jesse.

BOOK III

PSALM 73

THE FALSE HAPPINESS OF THE WICKED

1.   A psalm of Asaph.

        Truly, God is good to Israel,
        to those who are pure in heart.
2.   But as for me, my feet had almost slipped,
        my foothold had nearly given way.
3.   For I envied the arrogant,
        when I saw the prosperity of the wicked.
4.   They have no pangs at death;
        their body is sound.
5.   They are free from the sorrows common to man;
        they are not afflicted like other people.
6.   Therefore they wear pride as a necklace;
        they clothe themselves with a mantle of violence.
7.   Their eyes peep through folds of fat;
        the conceit of their mind knows no limit.
8.   They scoff, they speak with malice;
        from their high position they plan oppression.
9.   They set their mouths against heaven,
        their tongue roams over the earth.
10.   Therefore His own people turn to [follow] them,
        and drain to the dregs their abundant waters.[*]
11.   They say, "How could God know?
        Does the Most High have knowledge?"
12.   Look at these wicked men,
        always at ease, piling up wealth.
13.   Surely, in vain have I kept my heart pure,
        and washed my hands in innocence,
14.   when all day long I am afflicted with pain,
        every morning I suffer further punishment.

---

[*]   Swallowing thirstily the philosophy of the ungodly.

15. Had I decided to speak out in this fashion
     I would be betraying the generation of Your children.
16. So I tried to understand it all,
     but it was too much for me,
17. until I entered God's sanctuary;
     then I perceived what their destiny would be.
18. You set them on a slippery road,
     and hurl them to destruction.
19. How suddenly they are ruined,
     wiped out, destroyed by terrors!
20. As a dream vanishes when one awakes,
     so You, LORD, when You arise, will despise their image.

21. Long was my mind in ferment
     and my feelings in turmoil;*
22. I was stupid and ignorant,
     I was like a beast in Your sight.
23. Yet I am always with You,
     You hold my right hand.
24. You guide me with Your counsel;
     and in the end You will receive me with glory.
25. Whom else have I in heaven?
     And having You, I desire nothing else on earth.
26   Though my body and mind fail,
     yet God is the rock of my heart
     and my portion for ever.
27. For those who are far from You are lost;
     You destroy all who are unfaithful to You.
28. But as for me, my chief good is to be near to God;
     so I have made the LORD God my refuge,
     that I may tell of all Your works.

---

*   Lit. 'were pierced'.

PSALM 74

LAMENT ON THE DESTRUCTION OF THE TEMPLE

1.   A *maskil* of Asaph.

God, why have You cast us off for ever?
Why does Your anger continue to smoulder
against the sheep of Your pasture?

2.   Remember the community You made Yours long ago,
the tribe You redeemed as Your inheritance,
Mount Zion, which You made as Your abode.

3.   Direct Your steps toward the terrible desolations;
[see] all the havoc the enemy has wrought in the sanctuary.

4.   Your foes roar in Your meeting-place,
they have set up their standards as signs [of victory].

5.   It looked as though they had been wielding axes
upon the intricate woodwork,

6.   and then hacking away at its carved work
with pick and hatchet.

7.   They set fire to Your sanctuary;
they profanely razed to the ground
the dwelling-place sacred to Your name.

8.   They said to themselves, "We will utterly crush them,"
and they burnt all God's meeting-places in the land.

9.   No sign has come to us;
no prophets are left;
no one among us knows how long will this last.

10.   How much longer, God, will the foe blaspheme?
Will the enemy insult Your name for ever?

11.   Why do You hold back Your hand, Your right hand?
[Draw it] out of Your bosom, and destroy them.

12.   Yet God is my King from of old,
who brings deliverance throughout the land.

13.   It was You who split the sea by Your power,
    and shattered the heads of the monsters in the sea.
14.   It was You who crushed the heads of Leviathan,
    and gave them as food to seafaring men.[*]
15.   It was You who opened springs and streams [in the desert];
    and dried up ever-flowing rivers.
16.   The day is Yours and the night is Yours;
    it was You who set in place the moon[**] and the sun;
17.   it was You who fixed the boundaries of the earth;
    summer and winter, You created them both.

18.   Remember this, LORD; how the enemy blasphemes You!
    How vile people insult Your name!
19.   Do not deliver Your turtle-dove to the wild beasts;
    do not forget the lives of Your afflicted people for ever.
20.   Look to the Covenant;
    for all the dark places in the land are haunts of violence.
21.   Let not the downtrodden turn away in shame;
    let the poor and the needy praise Your name.
22.   Arise, LORD! Defend Your cause!
    Remember how vile men taunt You all day long.
23.   Do not forget the clamour of Your foes,
    the ever-rising uproar of Your adversaries.

---

[*]   Or: to the sharks.
[**]   So Targum.

PSALM 75

GOD THE RIGHTEOUS JUDGE

1. For the Chief Musician; set to *Al tasheth*. A psalm of Asaph.
    A song.

2. We praise You, God, we praise You,
    for Your name is near to us;
    men have told us of Your wonderful deeds.

3. When I set the appointed time
    I will judge with absolute fairness.
4. Though the earth and all its inhabitants melt away,
    I still hold its pillars firm.   *Selah*
5. To the boastful I say, "Do not boast,"
    and to the wicked, "Do not flaunt your strength."*

6. Do not flaunt your strength against heaven;
    or speak with insolent arrogance.
7. No influence from the east or from the west
    or from the wilderness can exalt man,
8. but it is God who gives judgement:
    one man He brings down, another He exalts.
9. For in the hand of the LORD there is a cup,
    full of foaming wine, mixed with spices;
    from this He pours,
    and all the wicked of the earth must drink
    and drain it to the very dregs.

10. As for me, I will declare [His glory] for ever;
    I will sing praises to the God of Jacob.
11. I will cut down the power** of evil men,
    but the power*** of the righteous shall be raised high.

---

* Lit. 'Do not lift up your horn.'
** Lit. 'the horns'.

PSALM 76

AN ODE TO GOD THE AWE-INSPIRING

1.   For the Chief Musician, with stringed instruments. A psalm
   of Asaph. A song.

2.   God is renowned in Judah,
   His name is great in Israel.
3.   His tent is in Salem,
   His dwelling-place in Zion.
4.   There He broke the fiery arrows of the bow,
   the shield, the sword and the weapons of war.   *Selah*

5.   You, LORD, were resplendent and majestic
   on the mountains of prey.
6.   Stout-hearted men were despoiled;
   they slept their last sleep;
   the valiant could not lift a hand.
7.   At Your rebuke, O God of Jacob,
   horse and chariot lay still.

8.   You, You alone are terrifying!
   Who can stand before You
   once Your anger is roused?
9.   From heaven You pronounced the sentence;
   the earth was afraid and kept silent,
10.   as God arose to judge,
   to save all the humble of the earth.   *Selah*

11.   When the fury of man will [turn to] praise You,
   You will, on Your part, hold back all that remains
   of Your fierce anger.

***   *Ibid.*

12. Make vows to the LORD your God and fulfil them;
    let all who are around Him bring tribute
    to His dread majesty.

13. For He curbs the spirit of princes;
    He is the terror of the kings on earth.

PSALM 77

COMFORT IN TIME OF DISTRESS

1.   For the Chief Musician. To *Jeduthun*. A psalm of Asaph.

2.   I cry aloud to God,
            I cry aloud to God that He may hear me.

3.   In the day of my distress I seek the LORD;
            at night my hand is stretched out unceasingly [in prayer];
            my soul refuses to be comforted.

4.   I think of God, and groan,
            I complain, and my spirit faints.   *Selah*

5.   You have kept my eyes from closing;[*]
            I am distraught, I cannot speak.

6.   I thought of the days of old,
            of the years long past.

7.   I remember at night my songs of praise;
            now I ponder in my heart, and my spirit searches for an
            answer:

8.   "Will the LORD reject for ever,
            and never again show favour?

9.   Has His love vanished for ever?
            Has His promise failed for evermore?

10.   Has God forgotten to show pity?
            Has He in anger withheld His compassion?"   *Selah*

11.   I concluded, "It was but to scare me,[**]
            that the right hand of the Most High has changed."

12.   I recall the deeds of the LORD,
            I recall Your wonderful acts of old.

13.   I meditate on all Your works
            and ponder on Your acts.

---

[*]   Lit. 'You hold fast my eyelids'.

[**]   So according to Rashi.

14. O God, Your way is holy;
    what god is as great as our God?
15. You are the God who works wonders;
    You have shown Your power among the nations.

16. With Your arm You redeemed Your people,
    the children of Jacob and Joseph.   *Selah*
17. The waters saw You, God,
    the waters saw You and writhed;
    the very depths were convulsed.
18. The clouds poured down water,
    the skies thundered,
    Your arrows sped on every side.
19. The noise of Your thunder was like the rattling of wheels;
    lightning lit up the world;
    the earth trembled and quaked.
20. You made Your way through the sea
    and Your path through the mighty waters,
    though Your footprints could not be seen.
21. You led Your people like a flock
    by the hand of Moses and Aaron.

PSALM 78

THE LESSONS OF HISTORY

1.   A *maskil* of Asaph.

    Listen, my people, to my teaching,
    incline your ear to the words of my mouth.

2.   I will begin my discourse with a parable,
    I will expound hidden lessons of the past.

3.   What we have heard and know,
    and what our fathers have declared to us,

4.   we will not hide from their children,
    but will tell to the next generation:
    the praises of the LORD and His might,
    and the wonderful acts He performed.

5.   He decreed precepts for Jacob,
    and established the Torah in Israel,
    bidding our forefathers
    to make it known to their sons,

6.   so that the next generation might know it,
    the children yet unborn,
    and they in turn would tell it to their sons;

7.   charging them to put their trust in God,
    and not forget the works of God,
    but keep His commandments;

8.   and not be like their fathers
    a stubborn and defiant generation,
    a generation whose heart was not steadfast,
    and whose spirit was not faithful to God.

9.   [So it was with] the men of Ephraim,[*]
who, though well-equipped and armed with bows,
turned and fled in the day of battle.

10.   For they did not keep God's Covenant,
and refused to live according to His law;

11.   they forgot what He had done
and the wonderful acts He had shown them.

12.   He performed wonders in the sight of their fathers,
in the land of Egypt, in the fields of Zoan.

13.   He divided the sea and led them through it;
He made the waters stand firm like a wall.

14.   He led them with a cloud by day,
and all night long by the light of fire.

15.   He split rocks in the wilderness,
and gave them water to drink
as if drawn from the great deep.

16.   He brought out flowing streams from a rock
and made the water run down like torrents.

17.   But they continued to sin against Him,
defying the Most High in the desert.

18.   They wilfully put God to the test
by demanding food for themselves.

19.   They spoke against God and said,
"Can God spread a table in the wilderness?

20.   True, He struck a rock and waters flowed,
and streams gushed forth.
But can He also give bread,
or provide meat for His people?"

21.   When the LORD heard this He was enraged;
fire broke out against Jacob,
wrath blazed against Israel,

---

[*]   The early commentators, Rashi and Ibn Ezra, refer to an ancient
tradition, based on the verse in 1 Chr. 7:21, that the Ephraimites,
impatient with their long servitude in Egypt, left that land prematurely,
and set out on their own for the promised land. On the way they were
confronted by the Philistines in Gath and suffered a heavy defeat.

157

22. because they put no faith in God,
    no confidence in His power to save.
23. Nevertheless He commanded the clouds above,
    and opened the doors of heaven.
24. He rained down manna for them to eat,
    and gave them the grain of heaven.
25. Men ate the bread of angels;
    He sent them provision in plenty.
26. He stirred up the east wind in heaven,
    and drove the south wind by His might.
27. He rained meat on them like dust,
    winged birds like the sand on the seashore.
28. He made them fall in the midst of their camp,
    all around their dwellings.
29. So they ate and had their fill;
    He gave them what they craved for.
30. They were not yet done with their craving,
    the food was still in their mouths,
31. when God's anger flared up against them.
    He slew the sturdiest among them,
    and laid low their choicest young men.

32. Despite all this they went on sinning,
    and had no faith in His wonders.
33. So He ended their days like a breath,
    and their years in sudden terror.
34. When He brought death among them,
    they began to seek Him,
    they would repent and seek Him in earnest.
35. They remembered that God was their rock,
    God the Most High, their redeemer.
36. But they beguiled Him with their mouth,
    they lied to Him with their tongue.
37. For in their heart they were not true to Him,
    they were not faithful to His Covenant.
38. But He, being merciful, forgave iniquity,
    and would not destroy them.
    Many a time He restrained His anger,
    and did not give full vent to His wrath.

39.   He remembered that they were but flesh,
       a breath that passes and does not return.

40.   How often did they defy Him in the wilderness
       and grieve Him in the desert!
41.   Again and again they put God to the test,
       and demanded signs of* the Holy One of Israel.
42.   They did not remember His power,
       nor the day He redeemed them from the foe;
43.   how He displayed His signs in Egypt,
       His wonders in the land of Zoan.
44.   He turned their rivers into blood;
       they could not drink from their streams.
45.   He sent against them swarms of wild beasts
       which devoured them,
       and frogs which destroyed them.
46.   He gave their crops over to the grubs,
       their produce to the locusts.
47.   He destroyed their vines with hail,
       their sycamore trees with frost.
48.   He abandoned their cattle to the hail,
       their livestock to lightning bolts.
49.   He let loose upon them His fierce anger,
       fury, rage and misery,
       a band of destroying angels.
50.   He blazed a path for His anger.
       He did not spare them from death,
       but gave them over to the plague;
51.   He struck down every first-born in Egypt,
       the first fruits of their manhood in the tents of Ham.
52.   Then He led forth His own people like sheep;
       like a flock He guided them in the wilderness.
53.   He led them in safety; they feared nothing;
       while the sea closed over their enemies.
54.   And so He brought them to His holy territory,
       to the mountain which His right hand had won.

---

*   Or: 'set a limit to'.

55.   He drove out the nations before them,
        allotting to each [tribe] his portion by the line,
        and settled the tribes of Israel
        in the homes [of the dispossessed].

56.   They still tested and defied God Most High,
        and did not keep His decrees.

57.   They turned away, and were disloyal like their fathers,
        they were unreliable like a slack bow.

58.   They provoked Him with their high places,
        they aroused His jealousy with their carved images.

59.   God heard and was enraged;
        He utterly rejected Israel.

60.   He abandoned the tabernacle of Shiloh,
        the tent in which He dwelt among men.

61.   He let the symbol of His might go into captivity,
        His glorious [ark] into enemy hands.

62.   He gave up His people to the sword;
        so enraged was He with His heritage.

63.   Fire devoured their young men,
        their maidens had no wedding songs.

64.   Their priests fell by the sword,
        and their widows sang no dirges.

65.   Then the LORD awoke as from sleep,
        like a warrior recovering from wine.

66.   He beat back His enemies,*
        putting them to lasting shame.

67.   He rejected the tent of Joseph;
        He did not choose the tribe of Ephraim,

68.   but chose the tribe of Judah,
        mount Zion, which He loved.

69.   He built His sanctuary [high] like the high heavens,
        and firm like the earth which He established forever.

---

*   Or possibly: 'He beats His enemies in the back parts'; so according to
Targum and early Jewish commentators, an allusion to 1 Sam. 5: 6,9.

70. He chose David, His servant,
and took him from the sheepfolds;
71. He brought him from tending the ewes
to be the shepherd of His people Jacob,
of Israel His own possession.
72. He tended them with blameless heart;
with skilful hands he led them.

PSALM 79

A PRAYER FOR VENGEANCE

1.   A psalm of Asaph.

O God, the nations have invaded Your inheritance,
they have defiled Your holy temple.
They have made Jerusalem a heap of ruins.

2.   They have left the dead bodies of Your servants
as food for the birds of heaven,
and the flesh of Your faithful for the wild beasts.

3.   Their blood was shed like water around Jerusalem,
with none to bury them.

4.   We have become the scorn of our neighbours,
the mockery and derision of those around us.

5.   How long, LORD?
Will You be angry for ever?
Will Your indignation blaze like fire?

6.   Pour out Your wrath on the nations that do not know You,
and on the kingdoms that do not call on You by name;

7.   for they have devoured Jacob,
and laid waste his homeland.

8.   Do not hold against us the sins of past generations.
Let Your mercy hasten to our aid,
for we have sunk very low.

9.   Help us, God our Deliverer,
for the glory of Your name;
rescue us and forgive our sins
for the sake of Your name.

10.   Why should the nations say, "Where is their God?"
Before our eyes let it be known among the nations
that You avenge the blood of Your servants that was shed.

11.   Let the groans of the captives come before You,
and by Your strong arm release those condemned to death.

12.   Pay back into the laps of our neighbours sevenfold
          for the insults which they hurled against You, Lord.
13.   Then we, Your people, the sheep of Your pasture,
          will praise You for ever;
          from generation to generation we will recount Your praise.

PSALM 80

A PRAYER FOR THE RESTORATION
OF THE NATION

1.   For the Chief Musician; on *shoshannim*, a testimony. Of
Asaph. A psalm.

2.   Give ear, O Shepherd of Israel,
who leads Joseph like a flock!
You who sit enthroned on the cherubim reveal Yourself
3.   at the head of Ephraim, Benjamin and Manasseh.
Rouse Your might and come to our help.
4.   Restore us, O God;
make Your face shine upon us, that we may be saved.

5.   LORD, God of Hosts,
how much longer will You fume at the prayers of Your
people?
6.   You fed them with tears for their bread,
You have made them drink tears by the bowlful.
7.   You have made us a source of strife to our neighbours;
our enemies mock us to their hearts' content.
8.   Restore us, O God of Hosts;
make Your face shine upon us, that we may be saved.

9.   You brought a vine out of Egypt,
You drove out the nations and planted it.
10.   You cleared the ground for it;
it took root and filled the land.
11.   The mountains were covered with its shade,
the mighty cedars with its boughs.
12.   It extended its branches to the Sea,
its shoots as far as the River.
13.   Why have You broken down its walls,
so that every passer-by can pluck its fruit?

14.   The wild boar of the forest gnaws it,
and the creatures of the field feed on it.

15.   O God of Hosts, relent!
Look down from heaven and see;
take care of this vine,
16.   the stock which Your right hand planted,
the bough which You raised up for Yourself.
17.   It has been burnt by fire and cut down by [our enemies].
May they perish by Your fierce rebuke!
18.   Let Your hand rest on the man at Your right hand,
on the son of man whom You raised up for Yourself.
19.   Then we will no more turn away from You;
Grant us new life, and we will call upon Your name.
20.   Restore us, LORD God of Hosts;
make Your face shine upon us, that we may be saved.

PSALM 81

A FESTIVAL MEDITATION

1.   For the Chief Musician upon *Gittith*. A psalm of Asaph.

2.   Sing joyfully to God our strength;
        shout for joy to the God of Jacob.
3.   Raise a song, beat the drum,
        play the sweet harp and the lyre.
4.   Blow the ram's horn in that month
        on the day when the moon is covered up for our feast day;*
5.   for this is a statute for Israel,
        an ordinance of the God of Jacob.
6.   He ordained it as a decree upon Joseph,
        when He went forth from the land of Egypt.

        It was then that I heard words unfamiliar to me:
7.   "I removed his shoulder from the burden,
        his hands were freed from the builder's basket.
8.   In distress you called and I rescued you;
        I answered you from the cover of the thundercloud;
        I tested you at the waters of Meribah.   *Selah*
9.   Hear, My people, and I will admonish you;
        Israel, if only you would listen to Me!
10.   You shall have no strange god;
        you shall not bow down to an alien god.
11.   I am the LORD your God,
        who brought you up from the land of Egypt;
        open your mouth wide and I will fill it.

12.   But My people would not listen to Me;
        Israel would have none of Me.
13.   So I let them go after their stubborn hearts,
        to follow their own devices.

---

*   i.e. on Rosh Hashanah, which is always on the first day of the month,
    when the moon is not seen.

166

14. If only My people would listen to Me,
    if Israel would walk in My ways!
15. I would soon subdue their enemies,
    and turn My hand against their foes."
16. Those who hate the LORD would come cringing to Him,
    and their punishment would last forever.
17. But Israel* He would feed with the finest wheat;
    "I would satisfy you with honey from the rock."

---

* Lit. 'him'.

PSALM 82

JUDGEMENT AGAINST CORRUPT JUDGES

1. A psalm of Asaph.

    God stands in the divine assembly;
    among the divines* He delivers judgement.
2. How long will you judge unjustly,
    and show favour to the wicked?   *Selah*
3. Do justice to the poor and the orphan;
    vindicate the lowly and the destitute.
4. Rescue the poor and the needy,
    save them from the hand of the wicked.
5. But they neither know nor understand;
    they walk about in darkness,
    while all the earth's foundations are tottering.
6. I had said, "You are godlike beings,
    all of you sons of the Most High."
7. But no, you shall die as men do,
    and fall like any prince.
8. Arise, God, judge the earth;
    for all the nations are Your possession.

---

* These are the judges who are considered as God's agents.

PSALM 83

THE NATION'S PRAYER AGAINST A HOSTILE ALLIANCE

1.   A song, a Psalm of Asaph.

2.   God, do not be silent;
     do not be quiet,
     do not be still, O God.
3.   See, Your enemies raise a tumult,
     Your foes lift up their heads.
4.   They devise crafty schemes against Your people,
     they conspire against Your treasured ones.
5.   They say, "Come, let us destroy them as a nation;
     let Israel's name be remembered no more."
6.   With a single mind they take counsel together,
     they form an alliance against You –
7.   the clans of Edom, the Ishmaelites,
     Moab and the Hagrites,
8.   Gebal, Ammon and Amalek,
     Philistia and the inhabitants of Tyre;
9.   Assyria, too, is in league with them,
     giving aid to the descendants of Lot.   *Selah*

10. * Deal with them as You did with the Midianites,
     with Sisera and Jabin at the brook, Kishon,
11. who perished at Endor,
     and were spread over the field like dung.
12. Treat their nobles like Oreb and Zeeb,
     all their princes like Zebah and Zalmunna,
13. who said, "Let us take for ourselves
     the pasture lands of God."
14. My God, make them like thistledown,
     like chaff driven by the wind.

---

*   For the historical events referred to in vv 10-12 see Judges chs. IV-VIII.

15. As fire consumes a forest,
    as the flame sets the mountains ablaze,
16. so pursue them with Your tempest,
    and terrify them with Your storm.
17. Cover their faces with shame
    until they seek Your name, LORD.
18. May they ever be dismayed and terrified;
    may they perish in disgrace!
19. Then they will know that You –
    whose name is the LORD –
    are alone supreme over all the earth.

PSALM 84

LOVE AND LONGING FOR GOD'S HOUSE

1. For the Chief Musician; on the *gittith*. A psalm of the sons of Korah.

2. How lovely is Your dwelling-place, LORD of Hosts!
3. My soul longs and pines for the courts of the LORD;
    my heart and my body cry out for the living God.
4. Even the sparrow has found a home,
    and the swallow a nest
    in which she rears her young –*
    [but I yearn] for Your altars,
    LORD of Hosts, my King and my God.
5. Happy are they who dwell in Your house,
    ever singing Your praise!   *Selah*

6. Happy is the man who finds his strength in You!
    When their heart is set on the highways [to Zion],
7. even as they pass through the vale of Baca**
    they regard it as a place of springs,
    as if the early rain has covered it with blessings.
8. So they go from strength to strength
    till they appear before God in Zion.
9. LORD, God of Hosts, hear my prayer;
    give ear, God of Jacob.
10. O God, behold our shield [the King],
    and look upon the face of Your anointed.

---

*   This division of the words in this verse follows the Massoretic notation,
    which places the main pause at 'her young'. Cf. Ibn Ezra.

** An arid and inhospitable valley through which the pilgrims passed en
    route to Jerusalem. The name *Baca*, meaning 'weeping', is taken from
    a species of gum-exuding (weeping) tree, which grew along its course.

11. Better one day in Your courts
    than a thousand elsewhere,
    I would rather stand on the threshold of the house of my God
    than live in the dwellings of the wicked.
12. Truly, the LORD God is a sun and shield;
    the LORD bestows favour and honour.
    No good thing will He hold back
    from those who walk with integrity.
13. LORD of Hosts,
    happy is the man who trusts in You!

PSALM 85

A PRAYER FOR COMPLETE RESTORATION

1.   For the Chief Musician. Of the sons of Korah. A psalm.

2.   LORD, show favour* to Your land,
     restore the fortunes of Jacob.

3.   Forgive the iniquity of Your people,
     cover up all their sins.   *Selah*

4.   Withdraw all Your wrath,
     turn from Your fierce anger.

5.   Come back to us, God, our saviour,
     put an end to Your displeasure against us.

6.   Will You be angry with us for ever?
     Will You prolong Your wrath for all generations?

7.   Will You not give us new life,
     so that Your people may rejoice in You?

8.   LORD, show us Your true love
     and grant us Your salvation.

9.   I will hear what God, the LORD, has to say;
     He promises peace to His people, His faithful ones –
     but let them not return to folly.

10.   Surely His help is near to those who fear Him,
     and His glory will once again dwell in our land.

11.   Let love and truth meet,
     righteousness and peace embrace.

12.   Truth will spring up from the earth,
     justice will look down from heaven.

13.   The LORD will bestow prosperity,
     and our land will yield its fruit.

14.   Righteousness will go before Him
     as He sets out on His way.

---

* The verbs in verses 2-4 are in the perfect tense, which can describe either events of the past or express a fervid prayer. The latter alternative is adopted in our text.

PSALM 86

PRAYER IN TIME OF DISTRESS

1.   A prayer of David.

       Incline Your ear, LORD, and answer me,
       for I am poor and needy.

2.   Guard my life, for I am loyal [to You;]
       as You are my God, save Your servant
       who puts his trust in You.

3.   Have mercy on me, LORD,
       for I call to You all day long.

4.   Bring joy to the life of Your servant,
       for to You, LORD, I lift up my soul.

5.   For You, LORD, are kind and forgiving,
       full of love to all who call on You.

6.   Give ear, LORD, to my prayer,
       heed the cry of my supplications.

7.   In the day of my distress I call on You,
       for You will surely answer me.

8.   There is none like You among the gods, LORD;
       there are no deeds like Yours.

9.   All the nations You have made
       will come to bow down before You, LORD,
       and honour Your name.

10.   For You are great and do marvellous deeds;
       You alone are God.

11.   Teach me, LORD, Your way
       that I may walk in Your truth;
       let my heart be undivided in reverence for Your name.

12.   I will praise You, LORD my God, with all my heart,
       and honour Your name for ever.

13.   For great is Your love towards me;
       You have delivered my soul from the depths of Sheol.

14.   O God, proud men have risen against me,
a mob of ruthless men seek my life –
they have no regard for You.

15.   But You, LORD, are a God, compassionate and merciful,
slow to anger, and abounding in love and truth.

16.   Turn to me and show me favour;
grant Your strength to Your servant,
and save the son of Your handmaid.

17.   Show me a sign of Your favour,
so that those who hate me may see to their shame
that You, LORD, have given me help and comfort.

PSALM 87

IN PRAISE OF JERUSALEM

1.   A psalm. A song of the sons of Korah.

        On the holy hills stands the city which He founded.
2.   The LORD loves the gates of Zion
        more than all the dwellings of Jacob.
3.   Glorious things are said of you, O eternal city of God.
4.   When I mention Rahab* and Babylon to my friends,
        or even Philistia, Tyre and Ethiopia,
        [people say,] "This man was born there."
5.   But when speaking of Zion,
        [people say,] "One and all were born in her."**
        The Most High Himself establishes her.
6.   The LORD will record in the register of peoples:
        "This [follower of mine] was born in her."   *Selah*
7.   Then all shall declare in song and dance:
        "The source of all our blessings is in you [Zion]."

---

*   A poetic name for Egypt. The word means haughtiness, arrogance.
**   Ibn Ezra interprets verses 4 and 5 thus: Whereas the other nations
        occasionally produce one or two great men, Zion produces time and time
        again men of stature.

PSALM 88

A CRY FOR HELP

1.   A song, a psalm of the sons of Korah. For the Chief Musician; on *mahalath le-annoth*. A *maskil* of Heman the Ezrahite.

2.   O LORD, God who saves me:
By day I cry to You, and also by night;
3.   let my prayer reach You;
incline Your ear to my cry.
4.   For my soul is sated with troubles;
my life is on the verge of the grave.
5.   I am already counted with those who go down to the pit;
I have become like a man bereft of strength.
6.   I am abandoned among the dead,
like the slain who lie in the grave,
whom You no longer remember,
and who are cut off from Your care.
7.   You have put me into the deepest pit,
into the darkness, into the lowest depths.
8.   Your fury lies heavily upon me;
You have afflicted me with wave after wave [of trouble].
    Selah
9.   You have removed my friends far from me,
You have made me loathsome to them.
I am shut in and cannot get out.
10.   My eyes ache through affliction.
I call to You, LORD, every day;
I stretch out my hands to You in prayer.

11.   Will You work wonders for the dead?
Will the shades rise up to praise You?   *Selah*
12.   Will Your love be spoken of in the grave,
Your faithfulness in the realm of destruction?

177

13. Will Your wonders be known in the place of darkness,
    Your justice in the land of oblivion?
14. But I, I call to You, LORD, for help;
    my prayer greets You every morning.
15. Why, LORD, do You reject me?
    Why do You hide Your face from me?
16. From my youth I have been afflicted and been near to death;
    I have borne Your terrors,
    but am in constant fear [of further calamities].
17. Your fierce wrath overwhelms me,
    Your terrors are destroying me.

18. All day long they surround me like a flood,
    they completely engulf me.
19. You have put friend and companion far from me;
    my closest friends are darkness* [and the grave].

---

* Or, following Rashi: 'are withheld from me'.

PSALM 89

PRAYER FOR THE FULFILMENT OF
GOD'S PROMISES TO DAVID

1.   A *maskil* of Ethan the Ezrahite.

2.   I will sing of the LORD's loving-kindness for ever;
    I will make known with my mouth Your faithfulness
    to all generations.

3.   I declare that Your love stands firm for ever;
    [constant as] the heavens You established Your faithfulness.

4.   "I have made a Covenant with My chosen one,
    I have sworn to My servant David:

5.   I will establish your line for ever;
    I will build up your throne firm for all generations." *Selah*

6.   The heavens praise Your wonders, LORD,
    Your faithfulness, too, [is praised]
    in the assembly of the holy beings.

7.   For who in the skies can compare with the LORD?
    Who is like the LORD among the heavenly beings,

8.   a God greatly revered in the council of the holy ones,
    held in awe by all around Him?

9.   LORD, God of Hosts, who is like You?
    LORD, You are mighty; Your faithfulness surrounds You.

10.   You rule over the surging sea;
    when its waves mount high, You still them.

11.   You crushed the monster Rahab dead like a corpse;
    with Your strong arm You scattered Your enemies.

12.   The heavens are Yours, the earth also is Yours;
    You founded the world and all that is in it.

13.   It is You who created the north and the south;
    Tabor and Hermon hail Your name with joy.

14.   Yours is an arm endowed with power;
    Your hand is strong, Your right hand raised high.

15. Righteousness and justice are the foundation of Your throne,
love and truth go before You.

16. Happy the people who know how to acclaim You,
who walk in the light of Your presence, LORD.
17. They rejoice in Your name all day long,
and are exalted through Your righteousness.
18. Indeed, You are their glory and strength;
through Your favour our horn is exalted.
19. For our shield belongs to the LORD,
our king to the Holy One of Israel.

20. Once You spoke to Your faithful in a vision,
You said, "I have given help to a great warrior,
I have exalted one chosen from the people.
21. I have found David, My servant;
with My holy oil I have anointed him.
22. My hand shall be ready to help him,
My arm to strengthen him.
23. No enemy will outwit him,
no wicked man oppress him.
24. I will beat down his foes before him,
and strike down those who hate him.
25. My faithfulness and love shall be with him,
and through My name his horn shall be raised high.
26. I will set his hand upon the sea,
and his right hand upon the rivers.
27. He will say to Me, "You are my father,
my God, the rock who saves me."
28. And I will make him My first-born,
highest of the kings of the earth.
29. I will keep My love for him always,
and My Covenant with him shall endure.
30. I will establish his line for ever,
his throne to be as lasting as the heavens.

31.	If his sons forsake My law
	and do not follow My orders;
32.	if they violate My precepts
	and do not observe My commands,
33.	I will punish their transgression with the rod
	and their iniquity with lashes.
34.	But I will not withdraw My love from him,
	or belie My faithfulness.
35.	I will not violate My Covenant,
	or alter what My lips have uttered.
36.	Once and for all I have sworn by My holiness;
	I will not be false to David.
37.	His line will continue for ever,
	his throne will endure before Me like the sun;
38.	it will be established for ever like the moon –
	that faithful witness in the sky." *Selah*

39.	Yet You have rejected, spurned,
	and raged at Your anointed.
40.	You have renounced the Covenant with Your servant;
	You have defiled his crown in the dust.
41.	You have broken down all his walls
	and reduced his fortresses to ruins.
42.	All who pass by plunder him;
	he has become the scorn of his neighbours.
43.	You have raised the right hand of his foes,
	You have made all his enemies rejoice,
44.	You have also turned back the sharp edge of his sword,
	and have not supported him in battle.
45.	You have brought to an end his splendour,
	and hurled his throne to the ground.
46.	You have cut short the days of his youth,
	and covered him with shame. *Selah*

47.	How long, LORD?
	Will You hide Yourself for ever?
	How long will Your wrath blaze like fire?
48.	O remember how short my life is.
	Was it to no purpose that You created all men?

49.	What man can live and not see death,
	or save himself from the grasp of Sheol? *Selah*
50.	LORD, where are Your former deeds of love
	which in Your faithfulness You swore to David?
51.	Remember, LORD, the abuse hurled at Your servant
	that I have borne in my bosom from many people.
52.	[Remember,] LORD, the taunts of Your enemies,
	how they mocked Your anointed at every step.
53.	Blessed be the LORD for ever.
	Amen and Amen.

BOOK IV

PSALM 90

GOD'S ETERNITY AND MAN'S FRAILTY

1. A prayer of Moses, the man of God.

    LORD, You have been our refuge in every generation.
2. Before the mountains were born,
    before You brought forth the earth and the world,
    from eternity to eternity You are God.

3. You turn man back to dust,
    saying, "Turn from sin, you sons of man."
4. For in Your sight a thousand years
    are like yesterday that has passed,
    or like a watch of the night.
5. You sweep men away, and they are asleep in death.
    They are like grass which springs up in the morning;
6. yes, in the morning it sprouts and flourishes,
    but by evening it droops and withers.
7. For we are consumed by Your anger,
    and shattered by Your fury.
8. You have set out our iniquities before You,
    our hidden sins in the light of Your presence.
9. All our days pass away under Your wrath,
    we spend our years like a sigh.
10. Seventy years, then,* is the span of our life,
    or, given the strength, eighty years;
    at their best** they are but toil and trouble;
    for soon it is over, and we fly away.
11. Who knows the power of Your anger?
    Your wrath equals the reverence due to You.
12. Teach us to number our days rightly,
    that we may gain a heart of wisdom.

---

*   In consequence of God's fury life is limited to seventy years.
**   Or: 'most of them'.

185

13. Relent, LORD! How long [will You be angry]?
    Have compassion on Your servants.
14. Satisfy us in the morning with Your loving-kindness,
    that we may sing and rejoice all our days.
15. Grant us joy for the days You have afflicted us,
    for the years we have known misery.
16. Let Your actions be seen by Your servants,
    and Your glory by their children.
17. May the pleasantness of the LORD our God be upon us.
    Establish for us the work of our hands.
    O do establish the work of our hands!

PSALM 91

SECURITY UNDER GOD'S PROTECTION

1.   You who dwell in the shelter of the Most High,
   and abide in the shadow of the Almighty,
2.   I say [to you], on behalf of the LORD,
   who is my refuge, my stronghold, my God in whom I trust,
3.   that He will deliver you from the fowler's snare,
   from the destructive plague.
4.   He will cover you with His pinions;
   under His wings you will find safety.
   His faithfulness is your shield and buckler.
5.   You will not fear the terrors of the night,
   or the arrow that flies by day;
6.   the plague that stalks in the darkness,
   or the pestilence that ravages at noon.
7.   A thousand may fall at your side,
   ten thousand at your right hand;
   but you it will not reach.
8.   You have but to look around
   and see the punishment of the wicked.

9.   Because you [have said:] "The LORD is my refuge;"
   because you have made the Most High your dwelling,
10.   no evil shall befall you,
    no plague shall come near your dwelling.
11.   For He will charge His angels concerning you,
    to guard you wherever you go.
12.   They will carry you in their hands,
    lest you strike your foot against a stone.
13.   You will tread on lion and viper.
    You will trample on young lion and snake.

14.   "Because he desires Me, [says the LORD,]
    I will deliver him.
    I will set him on high, for he knows My name.

15.   When he calls to Me, I will answer him;
       I will be with him in time of trouble;
       I will deliver him and honour him.
16.   With length of days I will satisfy him;
       I will show him My salvation."

PSALM 92

MARVELLOUS ARE THE WORKS OF GOD

1.   A psalm. A song for the Sabbath day.

2.   It is good to praise the LORD,
        to sing psalms to Your name, Most High;
3.   to proclaim Your love in the morning,
        and Your faithfulness at night,
4.   to the music of the ten-stringed lyre,
        with the melody of the harp.
5.   For You have made me glad by Your deeds, LORD;
        I sing for joy at Your handiwork.
6.   How great are Your works, LORD!
        How very profound are Your plans!
7.   The brutish man cannot know it,
        the fool cannot understand it.
8.   Though the wicked flourish like grass,
        and all evil-doers thrive,
        it is only that they may be destroyed for ever.
9.   But You, LORD, are eternally supreme.

10.   Behold, Your enemies, LORD,
        behold, Your enemies perish;
        all evil-doers are scattered.
11.   But You have raised my horn high like that of a wild ox;
        I am anointed with rich oil.
12.   My eyes see the defeat of my adversaries,
        my ears hear the downfall of the wicked who attack me.

13.   The righteous shall flourish like the palm tree,
        and grow like a cedar in Lebanon;
14.   planted in the house of the LORD,
        they shall flourish in the courts of our God.

15. In old age they shall bear fruit;
    still full of sap, still fresh are they,
16. proclaiming that the LORD is upright,
    my Rock, in whom there is no wrong.

PSALM 93

GOD, THE RULER OF THE UNIVERSE

1. The LORD is King, He is robed in majesty;
   the LORD is robed, He is girded with strength.
   The world is firmly established, it cannot be shaken.

2. Your throne stands firm from of old,
   You are from all eternity.

3. The rivers have lifted up, LORD,
   the rivers have lifted up their voices,
   the rivers lift up their pounding waves.

4. But above the roar of the great and many waters,
   above the mighty breakers of the sea,
   the LORD on high is mightiest.

5. Your testimonies are most trustworthy;
   holiness adorns Your house, LORD,
   for days without end.

PSALM 94

A WARNING TO ISRAEL'S OPPRESSORS

1.   God of vengeance, LORD, God of vengeance, appear!
2.   Arise, O Judge of the earth;
    give the proud their deserts.
3.   How long shall the wicked, O LORD,
    how long shall the wicked triumph?
4.   They pour out a stream of arrogant words;
    all the evil-doers brag about themselves.
5.   They crush Your people, LORD,
    and afflict Your own heritage.
6.   They kill the widow and the stranger;
    they murder the fatherless.
7.   And they say, "The LORD does not see;
    the God of Jacob pays no heed."

8.   Take heed, you most stupid people;
    you fools, when will you be wise?
9.   Can He who implanted the ear not hear;
    He who formed the eye not see?
10.   Shall He who disciplines nations,
    and teaches mankind knowledge, not punish?
11.   The LORD knows the thoughts of man,
    that they are but an empty breath.

12.   Happy is the man whom You, LORD, discipline,
    and teach him out of Your law,
13.   giving him peace in days of trouble,
    until a pit is dug for the wicked.
14.   For the LORD will not abandon His people,
    nor forsake His own heritage.
15.   For justice shall again accord with righteousness,
    and all the upright in heart will follow it.

16.	Who will rise up for me against evil men?
	Who will stand up for me against wrong-doers?
17.	Had not the LORD been my help,
	I should soon have dwelt in the silent grave.
18.	When I thought my foot was slipping,
	Your love, LORD, supported me.
19.	When anxieties increased within me,
	Your consolations cheered my soul.
20.	Can a corrupt throne be Your associate,
	one that brings on misery by its decrees?
21.	They band together against the life of the righteous,
	and condemn the innocent to death.
22.	But the LORD is my strong tower,
	my God is the rock where I take refuge.
23.	He will repay them for their wickedness,
	and destroy them for their evil deeds.
	The LORD, our God, will destroy them.

PSALM 95

A CALL TO ISRAEL TO WORSHIP

1. Come, let us sing joyfully to the LORD,
   let us acclaim the Rock of our salvation.
2. Let us come before His presence with thanksgiving,
   and acclaim Him with songs of praise.
3. For the LORD is a great God,
   a great King above all gods.
4. In His hand are the depths of the earth;
   the mountain peaks belong to Him.
5. The sea is His, for He made it;
   and the dry land too, which His hands fashioned.
6. Come, let us bow down and kneel,
   let us bend the knee before the LORD our Maker.
7. For He is our God, and we the people of His pasture,
   the flock that is under His care.

     O that today you would listen to His voice!
8. Do not harden your hearts as at Meribah,[*]
   as on that day at Massah[**] in the wilderness,
9. when your fathers put Me to the test;
   they tried Me, though they had seen My work.
10. For forty years I loathed that generation;
    I said, "They are a people whose hearts go astray,
    refusing to know My ways."
11. Therefore I swore in My anger:
    "They shall never enter My resting-place."

---

[*]   See Exodus 17:7.
[**]   *Ibid.*

PSALM 96

A CALL TO ALL PEOPLES TO WORSHIP

1.   O sing to the LORD a new song,
      sing to the LORD, all the earth.

2.   Sing to the LORD, bless His name;
      proclaim His salvation day after day.

3.   Declare His glory among the nations,
      His marvellous deeds among all peoples.

4.   For great is the LORD, and highly to be praised;
      He is to be feared above all gods.

5.   For all the gods of the peoples are idols;
      but the LORD made the heavens.

6.   Splendour and majesty are before Him;
      Strength and glory are in His sanctuary.

7.   Ascribe to the LORD, O families of the peoples,
      ascribe to the LORD glory and strength.

8.   Ascribe to the LORD the glory due to His name;
      bring an offering and enter His courts.

9.   Bow down to the LORD in the splendour of holiness;
      tremble before Him all the earth.

10.   Say among the nations, "The LORD is King."
      The world is firmly established and cannot be moved;
      He will judge the peoples with equity.

11.   Let the heavens rejoice and the earth be glad,
      let the sea and all that is in it thunder;

12.   let the fields and all that is in them exult;
      then shall all the trees of the forest shout with joy

13.   at the presence of the LORD for He is coming,
      for He is coming to judge the earth;
      He will judge the world with righteousness,
      and the peoples with His faithfulness.

PSALM 97

THE MAJESTY OF GOD

1.   The LORD reigns, let the earth be glad;
       let the many islands rejoice.
2.   Clouds and thick darkness are around Him,
       righteousness and justice are the foundation of His throne.
3.   Fire goes before Him,
       and burns up His foes all around.
4.   His lightnings light up the world;
       the earth sees and trembles.
5.   Mountains melt like wax before the LORD,
       before the LORD of all the earth.
6.   The heavens proclaim His righteousness,
       and all peoples see His glory.
7.   All who worship images, who boast of their idols,
       are put to shame;
       bow down to Him, all you gods.
8.   Zion heard and rejoiced, the cities* of Judah were glad,
       because of Your judgements, LORD.
9.   For You, LORD, are supreme over all the earth;
       You are exalted far above all gods.
10.   O lovers of the LORD, hate evil!
       He guards the lives of His loyal ones,
       and delivers them from the hand of the wicked.
11.   Light is sown** for the righteous,
       and happiness for the upright in heart.
12.   Rejoice in the LORD, you righteous,
       and praise His holy name.

---

*   Lit. 'daughters'.
**   i.e. 'stored up' – so Targum.

PSALM 98

GOD THE VICTORIOUS KING AND JUST JUDGE

1. Sing to the LORD a new song, for He has worked wonders;
   His right hand and His holy arm have brought Him victory.
2. The LORD has made known His salvation;
   He has displayed His righteousness in the sight of the nations.
3. He has remembered His love and His loyalty
   towards the house of Israel;
   all the ends of the earth have seen the salvation of our God.

4. Shout for joy to the LORD, all the earth;
   break into songs of joy, and make music.
5. Make music to the LORD on the harp,
   on the harp with melodious song.
6. With trumpets and the sound of the horn
   shout for joy before the King, the LORD.
7. Let the sea and all within it thunder,
   the world and all who live in it.
8. Let the rivers clap their hands,
   the mountains sing together for joy,
9. before the LORD, for He comes to judge the earth.
   He will judge the world with righteousness,
   and the peoples with equity.

PSALM 99

GOD THE HOLY KING

1. The LORD reigns, let the peoples tremble;
   He is enthroned on the cherubim, let the earth quake.
2. The LORD is great in Zion,
   He is exalted above all the peoples.
3. Let them praise Your name as great and awesome.
   He is holy!
4. You are a powerful King, a lover of justice.
   You Yourself have established equity,
   You Yourself have wrought justice and righteousness in Jacob.
5. Exalt the LORD our God, and bow down at His footstool;
   He is holy!

6. Among His priests were Moses and Aaron;
   among those who call on His name was Samuel;
   they called to the LORD, and He answered them.
7. He spoke to them in a pillar of cloud;
   they kept His decrees and the law that He gave them.
8. O LORD our God, You answered them;
   You were for them a forgiving God,
   even though You punished their misdeeds.
9. Exalt the LORD our God, and bow down at His holy
   mountain; for the LORD our God is holy.

PSALM 100

A CALL TO PRAISE GOD

1.   A psalm of thanksgiving.

       Shout for joy to the LORD, all men on earth.
2.   Serve the LORD with gladness;
       enter His presence with singing.
3.   Know that the LORD is God;
       He made us and we are His,
       His people, and the flock of His pasture.
4.   Enter His gates with thanksgiving,
       His courts with praise;
       give thanks to Him, and bless His name.
5.   For the LORD is good,
       His love is everlasting;
       His faithfulness lasts through all generations.

PSALM 101

THE RULE OF CONDUCT FOR A KING

1.   Of David. A psalm.

        I will sing of [Your] love and justice,
        I will sing praises to You, LORD.

2.   I will give heed to the perfect way –
        when will it come to me?*
        I will walk with blameless heart within my house.

3.   I will not set before my eyes any vile thing.
        I hate crooked practices.
        Such shall not cling to me.

4.   Men of perverse heart shall be far from me,
        I will have nothing to do with evil.

5.   The man who slanders his neighbour in secret
        him I will destroy;
        the man of proud looks and haughty heart
        him I will not tolerate.

6.   My eyes are on the honest men in the land,
        to have them live with me.
        He who walks in the way of integrity
        shall serve me.

7.   No one who practises deceit shall live in my house;
        no one who speaks lies shall endure in my presence.

8.   Morning after morning I will destroy all the wicked of the land,
        ridding the LORD's city of all evil-doers.

---

*   Or: 'When will You come to me?'

PSALM 102

A PRAYER IN TIME OF DISTRESS

1. A prayer of an afflicted man who is overwhelmed by
   suffering and pours out his complaint before the LORD.

2. LORD, hear my prayer;
   let my cry for help, come to You!
3. Do not hide Your face from me in the day of my distress;
   turn Your ear to me;
   answer me quickly when I call.
4. For my days vanish like smoke;
   my bones are charred as in an oven.
5. My heart is blighted and withered like grass;
   I neglect to eat my food.
6. Because of my loud groaning
   my bones cling to my flesh.
7. I am like a pelican in the wilderness,
   like an owl among ruins.
8. I lie awake; I am like a lone bird on a rooftop.
9. All day long my enemies revile me;
   those who mock me use my name as a curse.
10. I have eaten ashes for bread,
    and mingled my drink with tears.
11. In Your wrath and fury
    You lifted me high only to cast me down.
12. My days are like a declining shadow;
    I wither away like grass.

13. But You, LORD, are enthroned for ever,
    Your renown endures through all ages.
14. You will arise and have compassion on Zion,
    for it is time to be gracious to her;
    the appointed time has come.
15. For Your servants love her very stones,
    they cherish even her dust.

16. The nations will revere the name of the LORD,
and all the kings of the earth Your glory.

17. For the LORD has built Zion;
He has shown Himself in all His glory.

18. He heeds the prayer of the destitute,
and does not despise their prayer.

19. May this be written down for a coming generation,
that people yet unborn may praise the LORD.

20. For the LORD looks down from His holy height;
from heaven He surveys the earth,

21. to hear the groans of the prisoner,
to set free those condemned to death.

22. And so the fame of the LORD will be talked about in Zion,
and His praise in Jerusalem,

23. when the nations are gathered together,
and also the kingdoms, to serve the LORD.

24. He has weakened my strength in mid-course,
He has cut short my days.

25. I say, "O my God, do not take me away
when only half my days are done,
You, whose years go on through all generations."

26. Long ago You founded the earth,
and the heavens are the work of Your hands.

27. They will perish, but You remain;
they will all wear out like a garment;
like clothing You will change them, and they will vanish.

28. But You are always the same, and Your years never end.

29. The children of Your servants will dwell securely,
and their descendants will be established in Your presence.

PSALM 103

THE INFINITE GOODNESS OF GOD

1.   Of David.

     Bless the LORD, O my soul;
     let all my being [bless] His holy name.

2.   Bless the LORD, O my soul,
     and never forget all His benefits.

3.   He forgives all your sins,
     He heals all your ills.

4.   He redeems your life from the pit;
     He crowns you with love and compassion.

5.   He satisfies the prime* of your life with good things;
     your youth is renewed like the eagle's.

6.   The LORD executes righteousness
     and justice for all who are oppressed.

7.   He made known His ways to Moses,
     His deeds to the people of Israel.

8.   The LORD is compassionate and gracious,
     slow to anger, and abounding in love.

9.   He will not always rage,
     or nurse His anger for ever.

10.   He has not dealt with us as our sins deserve,
     nor requited us according to our iniquities.

11.   For as the heavens are high above the earth,
     so great is His love towards those who fear Him.

12.   As far as east is from west,
     so far has He removed our transgressions from us.

13.   As a father has compassion on his children,
     so the LORD has compassion on those who fear Him.

14.   For He knows how we are formed;
     He remembers that we are but dust.

---

*   Or: your old age (Targum), your mouth (Rashi.)

15.	Man's days are as grass;
	he blossoms like a flower of the field.
16.	When the wind passes over it, it is gone,
	and its place knows it no more.
17.	But the LORD's loving-kindness is for all eternity
	towards those who fear Him,
	and His righteousness reaches out to the children's children
18.	of those who keep His Covenant,
	and remember to observe His precepts.
19.	The LORD has established His throne in heaven,
	and His kingdom rules over all.
20.	Bless the LORD, you His angels,
	mighty in power, who do His bidding,
	and obey His spoken word.
21.	Bless the LORD, all His hosts,
	you His servants who do His will.
22.	Bless the LORD, all His works,
	everywhere in His domain.
	Bless the LORD, O my soul.

PSALM 104

GOD THE CREATOR AND SUSTAINER
OF THE WORLD

1. Bless the LORD, O my soul!
   LORD, my God, You are very great,
   You are clothed in glory and majesty.

2. He wraps Himself with light as with a garment;
   He has spread out the heavens like a veil.
3. He has laid the girders of His chambers on the waters;
   He makes the clouds His chariot,
   and speeds along on the wings of the wind.
4. He makes the winds His messengers,
   fiery flames His ministers.
5. He established the earth on its foundations,
   so that it shall never be moved.
6. You covered it with the deep like a cloak;
   the waters stood above the mountains.
7. But at Your rebuke they* fled,
   at the sound of Your thunders they rushed away,
8. rising over the hills,
   flowing down into the valleys,
   to the place You appointed for them.
9. You set a boundary which they were not to pass;
   never again shall they cover the earth.

10. He makes springs break out in the valleys,
    their waters flow between the hills,
11. supplying drink to all the wild beasts;
    there the wild asses quench their thirst.
12. Nearby nest the birds of the air;
    among the branches they sing their song.

---

* i.e the waters.

205

13. He waters the mountains from His lofty chambers;
    the earth is sated with the fruit of His* work.
14. He makes grass grow for the cattle,
    and vegetation for man's needs,
    that he may produce bread from the earth,
15. and wine to cheer the heart of man;
    oil to make his face shine,
    and bread to strengthen man's heart.
16. The trees of the LORD are well-watered,
    so, too, the cedars of Lebanon which He planted.
17. There the birds build their nests;
    the stork has its home on the fir trees.
18. The high mountains are for the wild goats,
    the crags are a shelter for the badgers.

19. He made the moon to mark the seasons;
    the sun knows the time of its setting.
20. You bring on darkness and it is night;
    then all the beasts of the forest are astir.
21. The young lions roar for their prey,
    seeking their food from God.
22. When the sun rises they stalk away,
    and lie down in their dens.
23. Then man goes to his work,
    and to his labour until evening.

24. How manifold are Your works, LORD!
    You made them all with wisdom;
    the earth is full of Your creations.
25. There is the sea, vast and wide,
    teeming with countless creatures,
    large and small alike.
26. There ships go to and fro,
    Leviathan also, which You formed to sport with.
27. They all look expectantly to You,
    to give them their food in due season.

---

* Heb. 'Your'.

28. When You give it to them, they gather it up;
when You open Your hand, they are well satisfied.
29. When You hide Your face, they are dismayed;
when You take away their breath, they perish,
and return to dust.
30. When You send back Your spirit, they are created anew,
and You give new life to the earth.

31. May the glory of the LORD endure for ever;
may the LORD rejoice in His works!
32. When He looks at the earth, it trembles;
when He touches the mountains, they pour forth smoke.
33. As long as I live I will sing to the LORD;
I will chant praises to my God all my life.
34. May my meditation be pleasing to Him;
I will rejoice in the LORD.
35. May sinners disappear from the earth,
and the wicked exist no more!
Bless the LORD, O my soul.

Praise the LORD!*

---

* Hebrew *'Halleluyah'*. The Hebrew term is a musical direction given to the singer. It comes as a surprise to many to learn that the term *Halleluyah*, so frequent in the Jewish liturgy, is found only in the last fifty chapters of the book of Psalms.

PSALM 105

GOD'S CARE FOR HIS PEOPLE

1.   Give thanks to the LORD! Call upon His name;
   make known His deeds among the peoples.
2.   Sing to Him; sing praises to Him;
   speak of all His marvellous deeds.
3.   Take pride in His holy name;
   let the hearts that seek the LORD rejoice.
4.   Seek the LORD and His strength;*
   seek His presence at all times.
5.   Remember the miracles that He performed,
   His wonders, and the judgements that He pronounced,
6.   O descendants of Abraham, His servant,
   O sons of Jacob, His chosen ones.

7.   He is the LORD, our God;
   His judgements cover the whole earth.
8.   He remembers His Covenant for ever,
   the promise that He made to a thousand generations;
9.   the Covenant that He made with Abraham,
   the promise on oath that He gave to Isaac.
10.   He confirmed it as a decree to Jacob,
    to Israel as an eternal Covenant,
11.   saying, "To you I will give the land of Canaan
    as your allotted heritage."

---

*   'His strength' represents 'the Ark of God'; cf. Ps.78:61, 132:8.

12.	When they were but few in number,
	very few, and strangers in the land,
13.	wandering from country to country,
	from one kingdom to another,
14.	He allowed no one to oppress them;
	He rebuked kings on their account:
15.	"Touch not My anointed ones;
	do not harm My prophets."

16.	He called down a famine on the land,
	and cut off all supply of bread.
17.	But He had sent a man ahead of them,
	Joseph, who was sold into slavery.
18.	They pressed his feet into fetters,
	his neck was put in irons;
19.	until what he foretold came to pass,
	and the word of the LORD proved him true.
20.	The king sent and released him,
	the ruler of peoples set him free.
21.	He made him master of his house,
	ruler of all his possessions,
22.	with power to imprison princes at will,
	and to instruct the elders in wisdom.

23.	Then Israel came down to Egypt,
	Jacob came to live in the land of Ham.
24.	There God made His people very fruitful,
	more numerous than their foes.
25.	He turned their hearts to hate His people,
	to conspire against His servants.
26.	He sent Moses His servant,
	and Aaron whom He had chosen.
27.	They performed among them His wonderful signs,
	and His miracles in the land of Ham.
28.	He sent darkness and all was dark,
	and none disobeyed His word.*

---

*   i.e. the plagues carried out the tasks they were sent to do (Rashi.)

29. He turned their waters into blood,
and caused their fish to die.
30. Their land swarmed with frogs,
even in the royal apartments.
31. He commanded and there came a mixture of harmful creatures,
and lice too, throughout their country.
32. He turned their rain into hail,
with lightning flashing throughout their land.

33. He struck down their vines and fig-trees,
and shattered the trees of their territory.
34. He commanded and the locusts came,
and grasshoppers without number.
35. They devoured every blade of grass in their land,
and consumed the produce of their soil.
36. Then He struck down all the first-born in the land,
the first fruits of their manhood.
37. He led out His people, laden with silver and gold,
and among their tribes not one stumbled.
38. The Egyptians were glad when they left,
for the dread of Israel had fallen on them.

39. He spread a cloud to screen them,
and fire to light up the night.
40. They asked [for food], and He sent them quails;
He satisfied them with bread from heaven.
41. He opened a rock and water gushed out;
it flowed like a river in the parched land.
42. Mindful of His sacred promise
that He made to His servant Abraham,
43. He brought out His people with joy,
His chosen ones with songs of triumph.
44. He gave them the lands of nations;
they took possession of what other people had toiled for,
45. so that they might keep His statutes
and observe His laws.

Praise the LORD!

PSALM 106

ISRAEL'S CONFESSION OF SIN.
A PENITENTIAL PSALM

1. Praise the LORD.

    Give thanks to the LORD for He is good;
    His love endures for ever.
2. Who can put into words the mighty acts of the LORD?
    Who can declare all the praise due to Him?
3. Happy are those who act with justice,
    who do what is right at all times.
4. Remember me, LORD, when You favour Your people,
    count me among those who enjoy Your saving power,
5. that I too may share the welfare of Your chosen ones,
    rejoice in the happiness of Your own people,
    and take pride in Your heritage.

6. We have sinned like our forefathers;
    we have done wrong,
    we have acted wickedly.
7. Our fathers in Egypt did not appreciate Your miracles;
    they did not remember Your many acts of kindness,
    but they rebelled at the sea, at the Red Sea.
8. Nevertheless He saved them because of His name,
    to make known His power.

9. He rebuked the Red Sea and it dried up;
    He led them through the deep as through a desert.
10. He saved them from the hand of the enemy,
    and freed them from the grip of the foe.
11. The waters covered their adversaries,
    not one of them survived.
12. Then they believed His words,
    and they sang His praises.

13. But they quickly forgot what He had done;
    they would not await [the working out of] His plan.
14. They craved for food in the desert,
    and challenged God in the barren waste.
15. He gave them what they desired,
    but sent a wasting disease among them.

16. They grew envious of Moses in the camp,
    of Aaron, too, the holy one of the LORD.
17. The earth opened up and swallowed Dathan,
    and covered over the company of Abiram.
18. Fire blazed up among their company,
    and flames devoured the wicked.

19. They made a calf at Horeb,
    and bowed down to a molten figure.
20. They exchanged Him who was their glory
    for the image of a grass-eating ox.
21. They forgot God, their deliverer,
    who had done great things in Egypt,
22. wonders in the land of Ham,
    and awesome deeds at the Red Sea.
23. He would have destroyed them,
    were it not for Moses, His chosen one,
    who stood in the breach before Him,
    to restrain His fury from destroying them.

24. Then they spurned the most desirable land;
    they had no faith in His word.
25. They grumbled in their tents;
    they would not heed the voice of the LORD.
26. So He raised His hand and swore
    to let them fall in the wilderness,
27. to scatter* their children among the nations,
    and to disperse them throughout the lands.

---

* Lit. 'to make fall;' cf. Targum.

28. They attached themselves to Baal Peor,
   and ate offerings made to lifeless gods.
29. They provoked Him with their practices,
   and a plague broke out among them.
30. Then Phinehas stood up and executed judgement,
   and the plague was checked.
31. This was credited to him as a merit,
   for all generations, for ever.

32. They angered the LORD also at the waters of Meribah,
   and Moses fared ill on their account.
33. For they rebelled against His spirit,
   and he* spoke rashly with his lips.

34. They did not exterminate the peoples
   as the LORD had commanded them,
35. but they mingled with the nations,
   and learned their practices.
36. They served their idols
   which became a snare to them.
37. They even sacrificed their own sons
   and daughters to demons.
38. They shed innocent blood,
   the blood of their sons and daughters
   whom they sacrificed to the idols of Canaan;
   and the land was polluted with blood.
39. They became defiled by their actions,
   and were wanton in their behaviour.
40. So the LORD's anger blazed against His people,
   and He abhorred His heritage.
41. He handed them over to the nations;
   their foes ruled over them.
42. Their enemies oppressed them;
   they were crushed under their rule.

---

*   i.e. Moses.

43.   Time and again He rescued them;
        but they were defiant in their schemes,
        and were brought low by their guilt.

44.   Yet He heeded their distress
        when He heard their cry.

45.   For their sake He remembered His Covenant,
        and in His great love relented.

46.   He roused compassion for them
        in the heart of all their captors.

47.   LORD our God, save us!
        Gather us from among the nations,
        that we may give thanks to Your holy name,
        and glory in Your praise.

48.   Blessed be the LORD, the God of Israel,
        from eternity to eternity!
        And let all the people say, "Amen!"

    Praise the LORD!

BOOK V

PSALM 107

GOD SAVES MAN IN DISTRESS

1.   "Give thanks to the LORD, for He is good;
His love endures for ever!"

2.   Let the redeemed of the LORD say this –
those whom He redeemed from the hand of the enemy,

3.   and those whom He gathered out of the lands,
from east and west, from the north and from the sea.

4.   Some lost their way in the wilderness, in the wasteland,
finding no path to a town to live in.

5.   Hungry and thirsty,
their spirit began to fail.

6.   Then they cried to the LORD in their trouble,
and He rescued them from their distress.

7.   He led them by a straight way
to a city where they could settle.

8.   Let them give thanks to the LORD for His goodness,
and for His wonderful deeds for men;

9.   for He satisfied the thirsty soul,
and filled the hungry with all good things.

10.   Some were living in darkness and in gloom,
fettered in misery and irons,

11.   because they had rebelled against God's commands,
and spurned the counsel of the Most High.

12.   So He humbled their hearts with hardship;
they stumbled, and there was no one to help.

13.   Then they cried to the LORD in their trouble,
and He saved them from their distress.

14.   He brought them out from the darkness and gloom,
and snapped their bonds asunder.

15.   Let them give thanks to the LORD for His goodness,
      and for His wonderful deeds for men;
16.   for He broke down gates of bronze,
      and cut through iron bars.
17.   Some were fools, suffering because of their rebellious ways,
      and because of their iniquities.
18.   They loathed all food,
      and were near death's door.
19.   Then they cried to the LORD in their trouble,
      and He saved them from their distress.
20.   He sent His word and healed them,
      and delivered them from the pit of death.
21.   Let them give thanks to the LORD for His goodness,
      and for His wonderful deeds for men.
22.   Let them offer sacrifices of thanksgiving,
      and tell of His deeds with songs of joy.

23.   Others went down to the sea in ships,
      plying their trade on the mighty waters.
24.   They saw the works of the LORD,
      and His wonderful deeds in the deep.
25.   By His word He raised a storm,
      that lifted high the waves.
26.   They mounted up to heaven,
      they went down to the depths;
      their hearts melted away in their plight.
27.   They reeled and staggered like drunken men;
      all their skill was of no avail.
28.   Then they cried to the LORD in their trouble,
      and He delivered them from their distress.
29.   He stilled the storm to a whisper,
      and the waves were hushed.
30.   They were glad when all was calm,
      and He guided them to their desired haven.
31.   Let them give thanks to the LORD for His goodness,
      and for His wonderful deeds for men.
32.   Let them exalt Him in the assembly of the people,
      and praise Him in the council of the elders.

218

33. Sometimes God turns rivers into a wilderness,
    springs of water into thirsty ground;
34. the fruitful land into a salt waste,
    because of the wickedness of the people who lived there.
35. Sometimes He turns the desert into pools of water,
    the parched ground into flowing springs.
36. There He settles the hungry,
    and they build themselves a city to live in.
37. They sow fields and plant vineyards
    that yield a fruitful harvest.
38. He blesses them, and their numbers increase,
    and does not let their herds decrease.

39. And when people grow few and are brought low,
    through tyranny, affliction and sorrow,
40. He pours contempt on those tyrants,
    and makes them wander in a trackless waste.
41. The needy He lifts high out of trouble,
    and increases their families like flocks of sheep.

42. The upright see it and rejoice,
    while the mouth of wickedness is silenced.
43. Whoever is wise, let him heed these things,
    and ponder on the LORD's loving-kindness.

PSALM 108

A PRAYER FOR VICTORY

1.   A song. A psalm of David.

2.   [*] My heart is steadfast, God.
I will sing and chant praises;
indeed, it is my glory [to do so].^{**}

3.   Awake, O harp and lyre!
I will awaken the dawn.

4.   I will praise You, LORD, among the nations;
I will sing praises to You among the peoples.

5.   For Your love is higher than the heavens;
Your faithfulness reaches to the sky.

6.   Be exalted, God, above the heavens;
let Your glory be over all the earth.

7.   In order that those dear to You may be delivered,
save with Your right hand and answer me.

8.   God declared in His sanctuary that I would triumph;
I would divide Shechem,
and measure out the Valley of Sukkoth.

9.   Gilead would be mine, Manasseh mine;
Ephraim my chief stronghold, Judah my sceptre.

10.   Moab would be my washbasin,
over Edom I would fling my shoe;
I would shout in triumph over Philistia.

---

[*]   This psalm is composed of portions of two psalms in Book II. Verses 2-6 are a repeat of Psalm 57, 8-12, and verses 7-14 of Psalm 60, 7-14 with some slight differences.

^{**}   So Rashi.

11. But who will conduct me to the fortified city?
    Who will lead me to Edom?
12. Have You not rejected us, God?
    You no longer, God, go out with our armies.
13. Give us aid against the foe,
    for worthless is the help of man.
14. With God's help we shall triumph;
    it is He who will tread down our foes.

PSALM 109

APPEAL FOR HELP AGAINST VICIOUS ENEMIES

1.   For the Chief Musician. Of David. A psalm.

    God, to whom I offer praise, do not be silent.
2.   For wicked and deceitful men open their mouths against me;
    they speak against me with lying tongues.
3.   They surround me with words of hate;
    they attack me without cause.
4.   In return for my friendship they accuse me,
    yet I pray [for them].
5.   They repay me evil for good,
    hatred for my friendship.

6.   [They say:] "Appoint over him a wicked man [as his judge];
    let the accuser stand at his right hand.
7.   When he is tried, let him be found guilty;
    may his plea incriminate him.
8.   May his days be few;
    may another take over his office!
9.   May his children be fatherless,
    and his wife a widow!
10.   May his children be wandering beggars,
    seeking [bread] far from their ruined homes!
11.   May a creditor seize everything he has,
    and strangers plunder the fruits of his labour!
12.   May no one show him any kindness
    or take pity on his fatherless children!
13.   May his posterity be cut off;
    by the next generation may their names be blotted out!
14.   May the iniquity of his fathers be remembered
    before the LORD;
    may the sin of his mother never be blotted out;
15.   may they be continually before the LORD,
    till He cuts off all memory of them from the earth!

16. For he never thought of doing a kind deed,
    but persecuted the poor and the needy
    and hounded to death the broken-hearted.
17. He loved to curse – may the curse light on him!
    He would not bless – may blessing be far from him!
18. He clothed himself with cursing like a garment;
    may it enter his body like water
    and into his bones like oil!
19. May it wrap him round like the clothes that he wears,
    like the belt that he puts on every day!"

20. May this* be the punishment of my accusers from the LORD,
    and of those who speak evil against me.
21. But You, God my LORD,
    deal with me as befits Your name,
    deliver me in Your generous love.
22. For I am poor and needy,
    and my heart is deeply wounded within me.
23. I fade away like a declining shadow;
    I am shaken off like a locust.
24. My knees give way from fasting,
    my body is lean for lack of fatness.
25. I have become an object of scorn to them;
    when they see me they shake their heads.

26. Help me, LORD my God.
    Save me, in accordance with Your love,
27. that men may know that this is Your hand,
    that You alone, LORD, have done it.
28. So let them curse,
    but You will bless;
    let them rise up, only to be put to shame,
    while Your servant rejoices.
29. My accusers shall be clothed in disgrace,
    wrapped in their shame as in a cloak.

---

*   i.e. the curses enumerated above.

30.   I will greatly extol the LORD with my voice;
        in the midst of the throng I will praise Him,
31.   because He stands at the right hand of the needy
        to save his life from those who would condemn him.

PSALM 110

THE KING IS PROMISED VICTORY

1.   A psalm of David.

       The LORD said to my lord,[*]
       "Sit at my right hand,
       while I make your enemies your footstool."
2.   The LORD will extend your mighty sceptre from Zion,
       saying,
       "Hold sway over your enemies."
3.   Your people will offer themselves willingly in holy attire
       on the day of battle.
       You retain the freshness of your youth,
       like the dew that falls from the womb of the dawn.

4.   The LORD has sworn, and will not go back on it:
       "You are a priest for ever
       after the manner of Melchizedek."[**]
5.   The LORD is at your right hand!
       On the day when His anger is aroused,
       he[***] will crush kings.
6.   He will execute judgement upon the nations,
       he will pile up the corpses,
       shattering heads far and wide.
7.   He will drink from the stream by the wayside;
       therefore he will hold his head high.

---

[*]   i.e. God's chosen king.
[**]   The king and priest to the Most High God; see Gen. 14:18.
[***]   *Ibid.* (God's chosen king.)

PSALM 111

THE WONDERFUL WORKS OF GOD

1.   Praise the LORD![*]

     I will praise the LORD with all my heart
     in the company and the assembly of the upright.

2.   Great are the works of the LORD,
     sought by all who delight in them.

3.   Glorious and majestic are His deeds;
     His righteousness endures for ever.

4.   He has won renown for His marvellous deeds;
     the LORD is gracious and compassionate.

5.   He gives food to those who fear Him;
     He keeps His Covenant ever in mind.

6.   He showed His people His powerful works,
     by giving them the lands of other nations.

7.   His handiwork is truth and justice;
     all His precepts are trustworthy.

8.   They are valid for ever and ever,
     enacted in truth and equity.

9.   He sent freedom to His people;
     He ordained His Covenant for all time;
     holy and awe-inspiring is His name.

10.   The fear of the LORD is the essence of wisdom;
     all who live by it show good judgement.
     His praise endures for ever.

---

[*]   An alphabetical psalm, of twenty-two lines, corresponding to the twenty-two letters of the alphabet.

PSALM 112

THE BLESSINGS OF THE UPRIGHT MAN

1. Happy* is the man who fears the LORD,
   who finds great delight in His commandments.
2. His descendants will be mighty in the land,
   a generation of upright men worthy of blessing.
3. Wealth and riches are in his house,
   and his righteousness endures for ever.
4. Even in darkness light shines for the upright;
   he is gracious, compassionate and kind.
5. All goes well with the man who lends graciously,
   who conducts his affairs with fairness.
6. Surely he shall never be shaken;
   the righteous man will be remembered for ever.
7. Bad news will have no terrors for him;
   his heart is steadfast, he trusts in the LORD.
8. His heart is firm, he has no fears;
   in the end he will see the downfall of his enemies.
9. He is lavish with his gifts to the needy;
   his righteousness endures for ever;
   his dignity** rises high in honour.
10. The wicked man shall see it and be infuriated,
    he will gnash his teeth and slink away;
    the desire of the wicked will come to nothing.

---

* An alphabetical psalm of twenty-two lines, corresponding to the twenty-two letters of the alphabet.

** Lit. 'horn'.

PSALM 113

GOD CARES FOR THE LONELY

1.   Praise the LORD!

      Praise, O servants of the LORD,
      praise the name of the LORD.

2.   May the name of the LORD be blessed
      now and for evermore.

3.   From the rising of the sun to its setting
      the name of the LORD is praised.

4.   High above all nations is the LORD;
      His glory is above the heavens.

5.   Who is like the LORD our God,
      enthroned so high,

6.   yet deigns to look down
      on heaven and on earth?

7.   He lifts the poor from the dust,
      raises the needy from the dunghill,

8.   to seat him with princes,
      with the princes of His people.

9.   He settles the childless woman in her home
      as a happy mother of children.

      Praise the LORD!

PSALM 114

THE WONDERS OF THE EXODUS

1.   When Israel came out of Egypt,
     the house of Jacob from a people of strange speech,
2.   Judah became His sanctuary,
     Israel His realm.
3.   The sea saw Him and fled,
     the Jordan turned back on its course;
4.   the mountains skipped like rams,
     the hills like young sheep.
5.   What alarmed you, O sea, that you fled?
     Jordan, why did you turn back?
6.   Mountains, why did you skip like rams?
     You hills, like young sheep?
7.   It was the presence of the LORD, the Creator* of the earth;
     it was the presence of the God of Jacob,
8.   who turns the rock into a pool of water,
     the flint into a flowing fountain.

---

*   So Rashi.

PSALM 115

LET ISRAEL TRUST IN GOD

1. Not to us, LORD, not to us,
    but to Your name give the glory,
    for the sake of Your love and Your truth.

2. Why should the nations say,
    "Where now is their God?"

3. But our God is in heaven;
    whatever He wills He does.

4. Their idols are silver and gold,
    the work of men's hands.

5. They have mouths, but cannot speak;
    they have eyes, but cannot see;

6. they have ears, but cannot hear;
    they have a nose, but cannot smell.

7. With their hands they cannot feel;
    with their feet they cannot walk;
    they utter no sound with their throat.

8. Their makers become like them;
    so, too, all who trust in them.

9. O Israel, trust in the LORD!
    He is their help and their shield.

10. O house of Aaron, trust in the LORD!
    He is their help and their shield.

11. You who fear the LORD, trust in the LORD!
    He is their help and their shield.

12. The LORD remembers us;
    He will give us His blessing.
    He will bless the house of Israel;
    He will bless the house of Aaron;

13. He will bless those who fear the LORD,
    small and great alike.

14. May the LORD grant you increase,
    you and your children.

15.   May you be blessed by the LORD,
the maker of heaven and earth.

16.   The heavens belong to the LORD,
but the earth He has given to man.

17.   It is not the dead who praise the LORD,
nor those who go down into silence.[*]

18.   But we will bless the LORD,
now and for evermore.

Praise the LORD!

---

[*]   i.e. the grave.

PSALM 116

THANKSGIVING TO GOD FOR HELP IN NEED

1.   I love the LORD,
for He hears my voice and my supplications;
2.   for He inclines His ear to me
whenever I call.
3.   When the pangs of death encircled me,
and the anguish of Sheol overtook me,
when I found nothing but distress and sorrow,
4.   I invoked the name of the LORD:
"I beg You, LORD, deliver my soul."

5.   Gracious indeed is the LORD, and just;
our God is full of compassion.
6.   The LORD protects the simple-hearted;
I was brought low and He saved me.
7.   Turn back, O my soul, to your rest,
for the LORD has treated you kindly.
8.   For You have delivered my soul from death,
my eyes from tears,
my feet from stumbling.
9.   I shall walk before the LORD
in the land of the living.
10.   I kept my faith,
even when I complained, "I am sorely afflicted,"
11.   even when I spoke rashly, "All men are deceitful."

12.   How can I repay the LORD
for all His benefits to me?
13.   I will raise the cup of salvation
and invoke the name of the LORD.
14.   I will pay my vows to the LORD
in the presence of all His people.
15.   Precious in the LORD's sight
is the death of His faithful ones.

16.   Truly, LORD, I am Your servant;
          I am Your servant, the son of Your maidservant;
          O free me* from my fetters.
17.   To You I will offer a sacrifice of thanksgiving,
          and invoke the name of the LORD.
18.   I will pay my vows to the LORD
          in the presence of all His people,
19.   in the courts of the LORD's house,
          in the midst of you, O Jerusalem.

Praise the LORD!

---

*   It is the precative perfect that is used here.

PSALM 117

WORLDWIDE CALL TO PRAISE GOD

1. Praise the LORD, all you nations,
    acclaim Him, all you peoples;
2. for strong is His love towards us,
    and the faithfulness of the LORD is everlasting.

    Praise the LORD!

PSALM 118

A PRAYER OF THANKS FOR VICTORY

1.   Give thanks to the LORD for He is good;
   for His love endures for ever.
2.   Let Israel say:
   "His love endures for ever."
3.   Let the house of Aaron say:
   "His love endures for ever."
4.   Let those who fear the LORD say:
   "His love endures for ever."

5.   In distress I called to the LORD;*
   the LORD** answered me, and gave me relief.
6.   With the LORD on my side, I do not fear;
   what can man do to me?
7.   With the LORD on my side as my helper,
   I will see the downfall of my enemies.
8.   It is better to take refuge in the LORD
   than to trust in man.
9.   It is better to take refuge in the LORD
   than to trust in princes.
10.   All nations surround me;
   by the LORD's name I will cut them down.
11.   They surround me, they surround me completely;
   by the LORD's name I will cut them down.
12.   They surround me like bees;
   they shall be extinguished like a fire of thorns;
   by the LORD's name I will cut them down.
13.   I was hard pressed*** so that I nearly fell;
   but the LORD helped me.

---

*   Hebrew 'Yah'.

**   *Ibid.*

***   Lit. You (i.e. each one of my adversaries) pressed me hard.

14. The LORD is my strength and my song;
    He has become my saviour.
15. Joyous songs and shouts of deliverance resound
    in the tents of the righteous:
    "The LORD's right hand has triumphed!
16. The LORD's right hand is exalted!
    The LORD's right hand has triumphed!"
17. I shall not die, but live,
    and proclaim the deeds of the LORD.
18. The LORD chastised me severely,
    but He did not hand me over to death.

19. Open for me the gates of righteousness
    that I may enter them and praise the LORD.
20. This is the LORD's gate,
    the righteous shall enter through it.
21. I will praise You, for You have answered me,
    and have become my deliverer.
22. The stone which the builders rejected
    has become the chief cornerstone.
23. This is the LORD's doing;
    it is marvellous in our eyes.
24. This is the day the LORD has made,
    let us rejoice and be happy on it.

25. We beg You, LORD, save us!
    We beg You, LORD, send prosperity!
26. Blessed is he who comes in the name of the LORD;
    we bless you from the house of the LORD.
27. The LORD is God;
    He has caused His light to shine upon us.
    With myrtle branches in hand,
    form the festal procession
    up to the horns of the altar.
28. You are my God and I will praise You;
    You are my God, and I will exalt You.
29. Give thanks to the LORD, for He is good,
    for His love endures for ever.

PSALM 119

IN PRAISE OF THE DIVINE LAW*

Aleph:
1.   Happy are they whose way is blameless,
    who follow the Torah of the LORD.
2.   Happy are they who keep His decrees,
    who seek Him with all their heart;
3.   who have done no wrong,
    but walk in His ways.
4.   You have commanded
    that Your precepts must be diligently kept.
5.   How I wish that my ways were steadfast
    in keeping Your statutes!
6.   Then I would never be put to shame
    when I regard all Your commandments.
7.   I will praise You with a sincere heart
    as I learn Your just laws.
8.   I mean to observe Your statutes;
    do not utterly forsake me.

Beth:
9.   How can a young man keep his way pure?
    By holding to Your word.
10.   I seek You with all my heart;
    do not let me stray from Your commandments.
11.   In my heart I treasure Your promise,
    for fear that I might sin against You.
12.   Blessed are You, LORD;
    teach me Your statutes.
13.   With my lips I repeat
    all the laws You have stated.

---

* An extended alphabetical Psalm. For each letter of the Hebrew alphabet there is a stanza of eight verses which all begin with that letter; thus there are twenty-two stanzas.

14. I rejoice in following Your decrees,
    as one rejoices over great wealth.
15. I meditate on Your precepts,
    and regard Your paths.
16. I delight in Your statutes;
    I will not forget Your word.

Gimel:
17. Deal kindly with Your servant,
    that I may live and keep Your word.
18. Unveil my eyes that I may behold
    the wonders of Your Torah.
19. I am a passing stranger on earth;
    do not hide Your commandments from me.
20. My heart is breaking with longing
    for Your laws at all times.
21. You rebuke the accursed proud
    who stray from Your commandments.
22. Remove from me scorn and contempt
    for I keep Your decrees.
23. Though princes sit together and scheme against me,
    Your servant studies Your statutes.
24. For Your decrees are my delight;
    they are my counsellors.

Daleth:
25. My soul lies in the dust;
    revive me according to Your word.
26. I confessed my ways, and You answered me;
    teach me Your statutes.
27. Make me understand the way of Your precepts,
    and I will meditate on Your wonders.
28. My soul weeps with grief;
    raise my spirits according to Your word.
29. Remove from me the way of falsehood;
    favour me with Your Torah.
30. I have chosen the way of truth;
    I have set Your judgements before me.

31.   I cling to Your decrees;
           LORD, do not put me to shame.

32.   I eagerly pursue the way of Your commandments,
           for You free* my heart [from anxiety].

He:

33.   Teach me, LORD, the way of Your statutes,
           and I will observe them meticulously.**

34.   Give me understanding that I may observe Your Torah,
           and keep it with all my heart.

35.   Guide me in the path of Your commandments,
           for that is my sole delight.

36.   Incline my heart towards Your decrees,
           and not towards love of gain.

37.   Turn my eyes away from worthless things;
           grant me life to follow in Your way.

38.   Fulfil for Your servant the promise
           which [You made] to those who fear You.

39.   Remove the reproach which I dread,
           for Your judgements are good.

40.   See, how I long for Your precepts!
           By Your righteousness grant me life.

Waw:

41.   May Your loving-kindness come to me, LORD,
           and Your deliverance, as You have promised.

42.   Then I shall have an answer for him who reviles me;
           for I trust in Your word.

43.   Do not utterly take away the true word from my mouth;
           for I put my hope in Your just rulings.

44.   I will always obey Your Torah,
           for ever and ever.

45.   I will walk about in all freedom,
           because I seek Your precepts.

46.   I will speak of Your decrees before kings,
           and shall not be ashamed.

---

*   Lit. 'broaden'.

** So Rashi. Others: 'to the end.'

47.   I find delight in Your commandments,
because I love them.

48.   I reach out my hands for Your commandments which I love,
and meditate on Your statutes.

Zayin:

49.   Remember the word [You spoke] to Your servant,
by which You have given me hope.

50.   This is my comfort in my suffering:
that Your promise gives me life.

51.   Though the arrogant bitterly mock me,
I do not swerve from Your Torah.

52.   I remember Your judgements of old, LORD,
and am comforted by them.

53.   Burning indignation grips me
because of the wicked who forsake Your Torah.

54.   Your statutes are the theme of my song
wherever I sojourn.

55.   In the night I remember Your name, LORD,
and I dwell upon Your Torah.

56.   This has been my merit,
that I always kept Your precepts.

Heth:

57.   [You are] my portion, LORD;
so I promise to obey Your words.

58.   I implore You with all my heart;
have pity on me according to Your promise.

59.   I have considered my ways,
and have turned my steps to Your decrees.

60.   I hasten, and never delay,
to keep Your commandments.

61.   Bands of wicked men prey on me,[*]
but I do not forget Your Torah.

62.   At midnight I rise to praise You
for Your righteous judgements.

---

[*] Following Rashi. Others: 'ensnare me'.

63.   I am a friend to all who fear You,
    to all who observe Your precepts.

64.   The earth is filled with Your loving-kindness, LORD;
    teach me Your statutes.

Teth:

65.   Do good* to Your servant, LORD,
    according to Your word.

66.   Teach me good sense and knowledge,
    because I believe in Your commandments.

67.   Before I applied myself** [to the Torah] I went astray,
    but now I heed Your bidding.

68.   You are good, and what You do is good;
    teach me Your statutes.

69.   Though proud men besmear me with lies,
    I observe Your precepts with all my heart.

70.   Their heart is gross like fat;***
    but as for me, Your Torah is my delight.

71.   It was good for me that I was afflicted,
    so that I might learn Your statutes.

72.   More precious to me is the Torah You proclaimed
    than thousands of gold and silver pieces.

Yod:

73.   Your hands made me and formed me;
    give me understanding that I may learn Your
    commandments.

74.   Those who fear You will see me and rejoice,
    for I put my hope in Your word.

75.   I know, LORD, that Your judgements are just,
    and in faithfulness You have afflicted me.

76.   O let Your love comfort me,
    in accordance with Your promise to Your servant.

77.   May Your mercies come to me that I may live,
    for Your Torah is my delight.

---

*   The perfect is taken in the precative, i.e. the imperative sense.

**   Taking the verb '*anah*' in the sense of being concerned or occupied
with, a meaning which is well attested in many passages.

***   i.e. they are callous and unfeeling.

78. May the proud be ashamed, for they wrong me with lies;
but I will meditate on Your precepts.

79. May those who fear You turn to me,
those who know Your decrees.

80. May my heart be blameless towards Your statutes;
then I shall never be put to shame!

Kaph:

81. My soul yearns for Your deliverance;
I have put my hope in Your word.

82. My eyes fail awaiting Your promise;
I say, "When will You comfort me?"

83. Though I have become [shrivelled]
like a wine-skin in the smoke,
I have not forgotten Your statutes.

84. How many are the days of Your servant?
When will You execute judgement on my persecutors?

85. The proud have dug pits for me,
in defiance of Your Torah.

86. All Your commandments are true;
men persecute me without cause; help me!

87. They had almost swept me off the earth,
but I would not abandon Your precepts.

88. By Your kindness grant me life,
that I may keep the decree that You uttered.

Lamed:

89. You, LORD, are eternal,
Your word stands firm in the heavens;

90. Your faithfulness endures for all generations;
You established the earth and it stands.

91. They stand today according to Your ordinances.
for all things are Your servants.

92. Had Your Torah not been my delight,
I should have perished in my affliction.

93. Never shall I forget Your precepts,
for by them You have given me life.

94. I am Yours; save me!
for I have sought Your precepts.

95. The wicked lie in wait to destroy me,
   but I ponder Your decrees.
96. I have seen that everything, however perfect, has a limit,
   but Your commandment is wide beyond measure.

Mem:
97. O how I love Your Torah!
   I meditate on it all day long.
98. Your commandments make me wiser than my enemies,
   for they are ever with me.
99. I have gained more insight than all my teachers,
   for Your decrees are my study.
100. I have more understanding than the aged,
   for I keep Your precepts.
101. I restrain my feet from every evil path,
   so that I may keep Your word.
102. I have not departed from Your ordinances,
   for You Yourself have taught me.
103. How sweet to my palate are Your words,
   sweeter than honey to my mouth!
104. I gain wisdom from Your precepts,
   therefore I hate every false way.

Nun:
105. Your word is a lamp to my feet
   and a light for my path.
106. I have sworn – and I will keep my oath –
   to observe Your just regulations.
107. I am sorely afflicted;
   LORD, preserve my life according to Your word.
108. Accept, LORD, the willing offerings of my mouth,
   and teach me Your ordinances.
109. Though my life is in constant danger,[*]
   yet I never forget Your Torah.
110. Evil men have set a trap for me,
   yet I do not stray from Your precepts.

---

[*] Lit. 'My life is continually in my hand.'

111. Your decrees are my everlasting heritage;
     for they are the joy of my heart.
112. I have resolved to carry out Your statutes;
     the reward is eternal.[*]

Samech:
113. I hate sceptics,^{**}
     but I love Your Torah.
114. You are my shelter and my shield;
     I await the fulfilment of Your word.
115. Away from me, you evil-doers,
     that I may keep the commandments of my God.
116. Support me as You have promised, that I may live;
     do not disappoint my hope.
117. Sustain me that I may be saved,
     and I shall always occupy myself with Your statutes.
118. You reject all who stray from Your statutes;
     for their scheming is in vain.
119. You discard as dross all the wicked of the earth;
     therefore I love Your decrees.
120. My flesh creeps from dread of You;
     I stand in awe of Your ordinances.

Ayin:
121. I have done what is just and right;
     do not abandon me to my oppressors.
122. Assure the well-being of Your servant;
     do not let the proud oppress me.
123. My eyes languish for Your deliverance,
     and for Your righteous promise.
124. Deal with Your servant according to Your true love;
     teach me Your statutes.
125. I am Your servant; give me insight,
     that I may know Your decrees.

---

*   Others conclude the verse: 'forever, even to the end'. See note on
     v.33.
** Or 'waverers'; i.e. those who are undecided and waver in their religious
     loyalties.

126.   It is a time for the LORD to act;
           for they have violated Your Torah.
127.   Truly I love Your commandments
           more than gold, even the finest gold.
128.   Truly I consider all Your precepts right in all matters;[*]
           I hate every false way.

Pe:

129.   Your decrees are wonderful;
           that is why I keep them.
130.   Your opening words shed light;
           they give understanding to the simple.
131.   I open wide my mouth, I pant,
           longing for Your commandments.
132.   Turn to me and be gracious to me,
           as You always do to those who love Your name.
133.   Direct my footsteps according to Your word;
           let no iniquity dominate me.
134.   Redeem me from the oppression of men,
           that I may keep Your precepts.
135.   Let Your face shine upon Your servant,
           and teach me Your statutes.
136.   My eyes stream with tears
           because men do not obey Your Torah.

Tsade:

137.   You are righteous, LORD,
           and Your judgements are just.
138.   You have imposed Your decrees with fairness;
           they are fully trustworthy.
139.   My zeal devastates me
           because my enemies ignore Your words.
140.   Your word is well tested,
           and Your servant cherishes it.
141.   I may be of little account and despised,
           but I do not forget Your precepts.

---

[*]   Or: 'I order my life in all things in accordance with Your precepts.'

142.   Your righteousness is an everlasting righteousness;
          Your Torah is truth.
143.   Though distress and anxiety have overtaken me,
          Your commandments are still my delight.
144.   Your decrees are ever just;
          give me understanding that I may live.

Qoph:
145.   I call with all my heart; answer me, LORD,
          that I may keep Your statutes.
146.   I call out to You: save me,
          that I may keep Your decrees.
147.   I rise before dawn and cry for help;
          I await the fulfilment of Your word.
148.   My eyes are awake before the night watches,
          to meditate on Your word.
149.   Hear my voice in accordance with Your constant love;
          grant me life, LORD, as is Your rule.
150.   My malicious pursuers are coming closer,
          they are far from Your Torah.
151.   Yet You are near, LORD,
          and all Your commandments are true.
152.   I have long known from Your decrees
          that You have established them forever.

Resh:
153.   See my affliction and deliver me,
          for I have not forgotten Your Torah.
154.   Defend my cause and redeem me;
          grant me life according to Your promise.
155.   Deliverance is far from the wicked,
          for they do not seek Your statutes.
156.   Great is Your compassion, LORD;
          grant me life, as is Your rule.
157.   Though my persecutors and foes are many,
          I have not swerved from Your decrees.
158.   When I see faithless men, I am disgusted,
          because they do not keep Your word.

159.   See how I love Your precepts;
       grant me life, LORD, according to Your love.
160.   The essence* of Your word is truth;
       all Your righteous laws are eternal.

Shin:
161.   Princes persecute me without cause,
       yet my heart fears only for Your word.
162.   I rejoice over Your promise
       like one who finds much spoil.
163.   I hate falsehood, I loathe it,
       but I love Your Torah.
164.   Seven times each day I praise You
       for Your just rulings.
165.   Great peace have they who love Your Torah;
       there is no stumbling for them.
166.   I wait for Your deliverance, LORD,
       and I fulfil Your commandments.
167.   My soul heeds Your decrees,
       for I love them dearly.
168.   I observe Your precepts and Your decrees,
       for all my ways are before You.

Taw:
169.   Let my cry come before You, LORD;
       give me understanding as You have promised.
170.   Let my entreaty reach You;
       save me according to Your promise.
171.   My lips shall pour forth praise,
       because You teach me Your statutes.
172.   My tongue shall sing of Your promise,
       for all Your commandments are righteous.
173.   May Your hand be ready to help me,
       for I have chosen Your precepts.
174.   I long for Your deliverance, LORD;
       Your Torah is my delight.

---

*   Or: 'the sum'.

175.   Let me live to praise You;
       may Your judgements help me.
176.   I have strayed like a lost sheep;
       come and seek Your servant,
       for I have not forgotten Your commandments.

PSALM 120

AGAINST TREACHEROUS FOES

1.   A song of Ascents.[*]

In my distress I called to the LORD
and He answered me.
2.   LORD, deliver my soul from lying lips,
from the deceitful tongue.
3.   What can the deceitful tongue give you?
What can it bring you?
4.   Nothing but the sharp arrows of a warrior,
and the burning coals of the broom tree!
5.   Alas, that I must dwell in Meshech,
that I must live among the tents of Kedar.
6.   Too long have I lived among men who hate peace.
7.   I am for peace;
but whenever I speak of it, they are for war.

---

*   See the Introduction where the names, technical terms and musical directions mentioned in the headings of the psalms are listed.

PSALM 121

THE LORD OUR GUARDIAN

1.   A song of Ascents.

        I lift up my eyes to the mountains;
        from where will my help come?
2.   My help comes from the LORD,
        maker of heaven and earth.
3.   He will not let your foot slip;
        He who guards you does not slumber.
4.   Indeed, the guardian of Israel
        neither slumbers nor sleeps!
5.   The LORD is your guardian;
        the LORD is your shade at your right hand.
6.   The sun will not strike you by day,
        nor the moon by night.
7.   The LORD will guard you from all harm;
        He will guard your life.
8.   The LORD will guard your coming and going,
        now and for evermore.

PSALM 122

GREETINGS TO JERUSALEM

1.   A song of Ascents. Of David.

        I rejoiced when people said to me,
        "Let us go up to the house of the LORD."

2.   Our feet now stand within your gates, O Jerusalem;

3.   Jerusalem, built up,
        like a city compacted together.

4.   There the tribes would go up,
        the tribes of the LORD,
        as was decreed for Israel,
        to praise the name of the LORD.

5.   There the thrones of judgement are set,
        the thrones of the house of David.

6.   Pray for the peace of Jerusalem:
        "May those who love you prosper;

7.   may there be peace within your walls,
        prosperity in your palaces."

8.   For the sake of my brothers and my friends,
        I will say, "Peace be within you."

9.   For the sake of the house of the LORD our God,
        I will pray for your well-being.

PSALM 123

A CRY FOR HELP

1.   A song of Ascents.

    To You, enthroned in heaven, I lift up my eyes.

2.   As the eyes of slaves look to their master's hand,
    as the eyes of a maid to the hand of her mistress,
    so our eyes look to the LORD our God,
    awaiting His favour.

3.   Favour us, LORD, favour us,
    for we have had more than enough of contempt.

4.   Too long have we suffered the scorn of the complacent,
    the contempt of haughty oppressors.

PSALM 124

GOD THE PROTECTOR OF ISRAEL

1.   A song of Ascents. Of David.

        If the LORD had not been on our side,
        – Israel may well say it –
2.   if the LORD had not been on our side,
        when men rose up against us,
3.   then they would have swallowed us alive
        in their fierce anger against us;
4.   the waters would have swept us away,
        the torrent would have surged over our heads,
5.   the raging waters would have surged over us.
6.   Blessed be the LORD, who did not leave us
        a prey for their teeth.
7.   We have escaped like a bird from the fowler's trap;
        the trap broke and we escaped.
8.   Our help is the name of the LORD,
        maker of heaven and earth.

PSALM 125

THE SECURITY OF GOD'S PEOPLE

1.   A song of Ascents.

Those who trust in the LORD are like Mount Zion,
which cannot be moved, but stands for ever.

2.   As mountains are around Jerusalem,
so the LORD is around His people,
both now and for evermore.

3.   Surely the rule* of wickedness shall not rest
in the land allotted to the righteous,
for then the righteous may set their hands to wrong-doing.

4.   Do good, LORD, to the good,
to the upright in heart.

5.   But those who turn to crooked ways,
may the LORD make them go the way of the evil-doers.
Peace be upon Israel!

---

*   Lit. 'sceptre'.

PSALM 126

SONG OF THE RETURNING EXILES

1.   A song of Ascents.

      When the LORD brings back Zion's exiles,
      it would be like a dream to us.[*]

2.   Then our mouths will be filled with laughter,
      and our tongues with songs of joy.
      Then shall they say among the nations,
      "The LORD has done great things for them."

3.   Indeed, the LORD will have done great things for us;
      we shall surely be glad.

4.   Bring back our exiles, LORD,
      like streams coming to the dry south.

5.   They who sow in tears
      will reap with songs of joy.

6.   He who goes out weeping, carrying a bag of seed,
      will come back with songs of joy, carrying his sheaves.

---

[*]   Or: 'We see it as in a dream.' Ibn Ezra.

255

PSALM 127

SUCCESS DEPENDS ON GOD'S BLESSING

1.   A song of Ascents. Of Solomon.

Unless the LORD builds the house,
in vain do its builders labour.
Unless the LORD guards the city,
in vain does the guard keep watch.

2.   In vain do you rise early and stay up late,
toiling hard for the bread you eat;
He provides as much for His loved ones in their sleep.

3.   Truly sons are a gift from the LORD,
the fruit of the womb is His reward.

4.   Like arrows in the hand of a warrior
are the sons of one's youth.

5.   Happy is the man who has his quiver full of them;
they shall not be put to shame
when they contend with the enemy at the gate.

PSALM 128

THE HAPPY HOME OF THE JUST MAN

1.   A song of Ascents.

    Happy are all who fear the LORD,
    who walk in His ways!

2.   You shall eat the fruit of your labour,
    you shall be happy and prosperous.

3.   Your wife shall be like a fruitful vine within your house;
    your sons like olive shoots around your table.

4.   And thus shall the man be blessed who fears the LORD.

5.   May the LORD bless you from Zion;
    may you see the prosperity of Jerusalem
    all the days of your life;

6.   and may you live to see your children's children!
    Peace be on Israel!

PSALM 129

AGAINST THE ENEMIES OF ISRAEL

1.   A song of Ascents.

Since my youth men have often attacked me,
– Israel can truly say so –

2.   since my youth men have often attacked me,
but they never prevailed against me.

3.   Ploughmen have ploughed across my back,
they made long furrows upon me.

4.   But the LORD is just,
He has snapped the cords of the wicked.

5.   Let all who hate Zion
be ashamed and driven back.

6.   Let them be like grass growing on the roof,
which withers before it can be pulled up;

7.   with which the reaper cannot fill his hand,
nor the binder of sheaves his lap,

8.   so that passers-by will never exchange greetings with them:
"The LORD's blessing be upon you!"
"We bless you in the name of the LORD!"

PSALM 130

A PRAYER FOR PARDON AND MERCY

1.   A song of Ascents.

       Out of the depths I call to You, LORD.
2.   LORD, hear my voice;
       let Your ears be attentive to my plea for mercy.
3.   If You, LORD, should keep account of sins,
       who could survive?
4.   But with You there is forgiveness;
       therefore You are revered.

5.   I wait for the LORD; my soul waits;
       hopefully I wait for His word.
6.   My soul waits for the LORD
       more eagerly than watchmen for the morning;
       yes, more than watchmen for the morning.
7.   O Israel, put your hope in the LORD;
       for with the LORD there is loving-kindness,
       and with Him there is great power to redeem.
8.   He Himself will redeem Israel from all their sins.

PSALM 131

HUMBLE TRUST IN GOD

1.   A song of Ascents. Of David.

        LORD, my heart is not proud,
        nor are my eyes haughty;
        I do not concern myself with matters,
        too great or too wonderful for me.

2.   But I have stilled and calmed my soul,
        like a weaned child with its mother;
        like a weaned child is my soul within me.

3.   O Israel, put your hope in the LORD,
        now and for evermore.

PSALM 132

THE PACT BETWEEN DAVID AND THE LORD

1.   A song of Ascents.

        LORD, remember in David's favour
        all the hardships he endured.
2.   How he swore an oath to the LORD
        and vowed to the Mighty One of Jacob:
3.   "I will not enter my house,
        nor will I mount the couch spread for me;
4.   I will give no sleep to my eyes,
        no slumber to my eyelids,
5.   until I find a place for the LORD,
        a dwelling for the Mighty One of Jacob."
6.   Then we heard that it* was to be at Ephrat,
        we learned that it was to be in the region of Jaar.**

7.   Let us enter His dwelling,
        let us worship at His footstool.
8.   Arise, LORD, and enter Your resting-place,
        You and the Ark [the symbol] of Your strength.
9.   Your priests are robed in righteousness,
        Your loyal ones sing for joy.
10.   For the sake of Your servant David,
        do not reject Your anointed one.

---

*   i.e. the Ark of God.

** David and his men discovered that the Ark and God's dwelling-place
were to be located in Jerusalem; the places named in this verse are in the
vicinity of Jerusalem: Ephrat (another name for Bethlehem) about six
miles south of Jerusalem, and Jaar (probably Kiriath-Jearim) about six
miles north of Jerusalem. Cf. B.T. Tractate Zebahim, 54b.

11.   The LORD swore to David,
a sure oath that He will not revoke:
"One born of your own body
I will set upon your throne.

12.   If your sons keep My Covenant,
and My decrees that I teach them,
then their sons also, to the end of time,
shall sit upon your throne."

13.   For the LORD has chosen Zion;
He desired her for His seat.

14.   This is My resting-place for ever;
here will I dwell, for such is My desire.

15.   I will amply bless her provision,
I will satisfy her needy with bread.

16.   I will clothe her priests with salvation,
and her loyal ones shall sing for joy.

17.   There I will make David's dynasty* to flourish;
I will prepare a lamp for My anointed.

18.   His enemies I will clothe with shame;
but on him his crown shall sparkle.

---

*   Lit. 'horn'.

PSALM 133

THE BLESSINGS OF BROTHERLY LOVE

1.   A song of Ascents. Of David.

How good and pleasant it is
to live together as brothers in unity!

2.   It is like precious oil poured on the head,
running down on to the beard,
like the oil on Aaron's beard,
which ran down on to the collar of his robes;

3.   it is like the dew of Hermon
that falls on the hills of Zion.
There the LORD bestows His blessing,
life for evermore.

PSALM 134

A CALL TO WORSHIP

1. A song of Ascents.

    Come, bless the LORD, all you servants of the LORD,
    who minister night after night in the house of the LORD.
2. Lift up your hands towards the sanctuary
    and bless the LORD.
3. May the LORD, maker of heaven and earth,
    bless you from Zion!

PSALM 135

HOUSE OF ISRAEL PRAISE THE LORD

1.   Praise the LORD!

        Praise the name of the LORD.
        Give praise, you servants of the LORD,
2.   who stand in the house of the LORD,
        in the courts of the house of our God.
3.   Praise the LORD, for the LORD is good;
        sing praises to His name, for it is pleasant.[*]
4.   For the LORD has chosen Jacob for Himself,
        Israel as His treasured possession.

5.   For I know that the LORD is great,
        that our LORD is above all gods.
6.   Whatever the LORD desires He does,
        in heaven and on earth,
        in the seas and in all the depths.
7.   He brings up mists from the ends of the earth;
        He makes lightnings for the rain;
        He brings out the wind from His storehouses.

8.   He struck down the first-born of Egypt,
        both of man and beast.
9.   He sent signs and wonders into the midst of Egypt,[**]
        against Pharaoh and against all his servants.
10.   He smote many nations
        and slew mighty kings:
11.   Sihon, king of the Amorites,
        Og, king of Bashan,
        and all the kingdoms of Canaan.

---

[*]   Or: for He is gracious.
[**]   'Into the midst of Egypt', so Rashi. According to Ibn Ezra: 'Into your
        midst, O Egypt.'

265

12. He gave their land as a heritage,
a heritage to His people Israel.

13. LORD, Your name endures for ever;
Your renown, LORD, throughout all generations.

14. For the LORD will vindicate His people,
and have pity on His servants.

15. The idols of the nations are silver and gold,
the work of men's hands.

16. They have mouths, but cannot speak;
they have eyes, but cannot see;

17. they have ears, but cannot hear;
neither is there breath in their mouths.

18. Their makers become like them;
and so do all who trust in them.

19. House of Israel, bless the LORD!
House of Aaron, bless the LORD!

20. House of Levi, bless the LORD!
You who fear the LORD, bless the LORD!

21. Blessed from Zion be the LORD,
who dwells in Jerusalem!

Praise the LORD!

PSALM 136

THE GREAT HALLEL. A HYMN OF THANKSGIVING

1. Give thanks to the LORD, for He is good;
    His love endures for ever!
2. Give thanks to the God of gods,
    His love endures for ever!
3. Give thanks to the LORD of lords,
    His love endures for ever!
4. To Him who alone works great wonders,
    His love endures for ever!
5. To Him who made the heavens with wisdom,
    His love endures for ever!
6. To Him who spread out the earth above the waters,
    His love endures for ever!
7. To Him who made the great lights;
    His love endures for ever!
8. the sun to rule by day,
    His love endures for ever!
9. the moon and the stars to rule by night;
    His love endures for ever!
10. To Him who struck Egypt through their first-born,
    His love endures for ever!
11. and brought out Israel from their midst,
    His love endures for ever!
12. with a strong hand and outstretched arm,
    His love endures for ever!
13. To Him who split apart the Red Sea,
    His love endures for ever!
14. and made Israel pass through it,
    His love endures for ever!
15. but Pharaoh and his army He drove into the Red Sea;
    His love endures for ever!
16. To Him who led His people through the wilderness;
    His love endures for ever!

17. To Him who struck down great kings,
    His love endures for ever!
18. and slew mighty kings,
    His love endures for ever!
19. Sihon, king of the Amorites,
    His love endures for ever!
20. and Og, king of Bashan,
    His love endures for ever!
21. and gave their land as a heritage,
    His love endures for ever!
22. a heritage to His servant Israel;
    His love endures for ever!
23. To Him who remembered us in our low estate,
    His love endures for ever!
24. and rescued us from our enemies,
    His love endures for ever!
25. To Him who gives food to all flesh,
    His love endures for ever!
26. Give thanks to the God of heaven,
    His love endures for ever!

PSALM 137

THE EXILE'S REMEMBRANCE OF ZION

1. By the rivers of Babylon we sat,
   weeping loudly, as we remembered Zion.
2. On the willow trees there
   we hung up our lyres.
3. For there our captors had asked us for songs,
   our tormentors called for merriment:
   "Sing for us one of the songs of Zion."
4. How can we sing the LORD's song
   on foreign soil?
5. If I forget you, O Jerusalem,
   may my right hand wither away;*
6. may my tongue cling to my palate
   if I do not remember you,
   if I do not set Jerusalem
   above my greatest joy.

7. Remember, LORD, against the Edomites
   the day when Jerusalem fell,
   how they cried, "Lay it bare, lay it bare,
   to its very foundations!"
8. O daughter of Babylon, you devastator,
   happy is he who repays you
   for what you did to us!
9. Happy is he who seizes your babes
   and dashes them against a rock!

---

* Or : 'forget its skill'.

PSALM 138

THANKSGIVING FOR GOD'S DELIVERANCE

1.   Of David.

I will praise You with all my heart;
in the presence of the mighty* I will sing Your praises.

2.   I will bow down towards Your holy temple,
and praise Your name for Your love and faithfulness;
for You have magnified Your word
above all Your Name.**

3.   Whenever I called, You answered me;
You inspired me with courage and strength.

4.   All the kings of the earth shall praise You, LORD,
when they have heard the words of Your mouth.

5.   They shall sing of the LORD's ways;
for great is the glory of the LORD.

6.   The LORD is exalted, yet He cares for the lowly;
from afar He takes note of the proud.

7.   Though I walk in the midst of trouble,
You preserve my life;
against the raging of my enemies
You wield Your power;
and with Your right hand You save me.

8.   The LORD will fulfil His purpose for me;
Your love, LORD, endures for ever.
Do not abandon the work of Your hands.

---

*   Or 'divine beings'.

** God's 'word' here signifies His promise. The sense of the verse is: As
truth is a characteristic of God's name (cf. Ps.31,6) one may be assured
that He will honour His pledged word, but in reality God has fulfilled
His promise to His people in a measure far in excess of all expectation.

270

PSALM 139

THE ALL-KNOWING AND EVER-PRESENT GOD

1. To the Chief Musician. A psalm of David.

    LORD, You have examined me, and You know me.
2. You know when I sit down and when I rise up;
    You discern my thoughts from afar.
3. You scrutinise* my walking and my resting;
    You are familiar with all my ways.
4. Before ever a word is on my tongue,
    You, LORD, know it all.
5. You have hemmed me in on all sides,
    and laid Your hand upon me.
6. Such knowledge is too wonderful for me;
    too high, I cannot reach it.

7. Where can I escape from Your spirit?
    Where can I flee from Your presence?
8. If I ascend to heaven, You are there;
    if I make my bed in Sheol, You are there.
9. If I take the wings of the dawn,
    and dwell at the sea's furthest end,
10. even there Your hand will be guiding me,
    Your right hand will be holding me fast.
11. Then I realised, "Even in the darkness He sees me;**
    even in the night there is light all around me."
12. For darkness is not dark to You;
    night is as light as day;
    darkness and light are the same.

---

*   Lit. 'You sift'.
** The root of the Hebrew word used here is *shuf*, which, like the Arabic
    root *shafa*, means: to observe or see.

271

13. It was You who created my inward parts;*
    You knit me together in my mother's womb.
14. I praise You because I am fearfully and wondrously made;
    wonderful are Your works; I know that full well.
15. My frame was not hidden from You,
    when I was made in the secret place,
    woven together in the lowest depths of the earth.
16. Your eyes saw my shapeless mass;
    all the days ordained [for me] were recorded in Your book,
    before one of them ever came into being.
17. How precious to me are Your thoughts, God!
    How vast their number!
18. Were I to count them, they would outnumber the grains of
    sand.
    Were I to finish the count, I must be like You [eternal].

19. If only, God, You would slay the wicked!
    Away from me, you bloodthirsty men!
20. They speak of You with wicked intent;
    Your adversaries swear by You falsely.
21. Do I not hate those who hate You, LORD,
    and loathe those who rise up against You?
22. I have nothing but utter hatred for them;
    I count them my enemies.
23. Examine me, God, and know my mind;
    test me, and know my innermost thoughts.
24. See if there be any grievous way in me;
    and lead me in the way everlasting.

---

* Lit. 'my kidneys'.

272

PSALM 140

PRAYER FOR DELIVERANCE FROM VIOLENT MEN

1.   For the Chief Musician. A psalm of David.

2.   Rescue me, LORD, from evil men;
     protect me from violent men,
3.   who devise evil in their hearts,
     and stir up wars day after day.
4.   They sharpen their tongues like a serpent's;
     spider's poison is under their lips.   *Selah*

5.   Guard me, LORD, from the hands of the wicked;
     protect me from violent men,
     who plan to trip up my feet.
6.   Arrogant men have hidden a trap for me;
     they have spread a net with its cords along my path;
     they have set snares for me.   *Selah*

7.   I say to the LORD, "You are my God."
     Hear, LORD, my cry for mercy.
8.   O God, LORD, the strength of my salvation,
     shield my head in the day of battle.
9.   LORD, do not grant the desires of the wicked;
     do not let their plans succeed,
     lest they exalt themselves.   *Selah*
10.   As for the leaders of those who beset me –
     let the mischief of their lips overwhelm them.
11.   Let burning coals drop down upon them,
     let them be cast into the fire,
     into miry pits, never to rise again.
12.   Let the slanderer have no place in the land;
     let disaster hound the violent man to destruction.

13.   I know that the LORD will maintain the cause of the poor,
      the rights of the needy.
14.   Surely the righteous will praise Your name;
      the upright shall live in Your presence.

PSALM 141

A PRAYER FOR PROTECTION

1.   A psalm of David.

    I call to You, LORD; come quickly to me.
    Hear my voice when I call to You.

2.   May my prayer be like an incense offering set before You,
    the lifting up of my hands as the evening offering.

3.   LORD, set a guard over my mouth;
    keep watch at the door of my lips.

4.   Do not let my heart turn to an evil thing,
    or take part in wicked deeds
    with men who are evil-doers;
    let me not eat of their dainties.

5.   If a righteous man strikes me, 'twere an act of kindness;
    if he reproves me, 'twere like choice oil,
    my head would not refuse it.
    But while I live my prayer is ever against their wickedness.

6.   When their rulers are cast down by the Rock,[*]
    then the people will listen to my words for they are pleasant.

7.   As when one harrows and breaks up the ground,
    so were our bones strewn at the mouth of Sheol.[**]

8.   But to You, God, my LORD, my eyes are turned;
    in You I take refuge; let not my life ebb away.

9.   Keep me from the trap which they have set for me,
    and from the snares of evil-doers.

10.   Let the wicked, one and all, fall into their own nets,
    while I pass on my way.

---

[*]   i.e the Almighty.

[**]   By the hands of those cruel rulers.

PSALM 142

A PLEA FOR HELP

1.   *A maskil* of David; when he was in the cave.[*] A prayer.

2.   I cry aloud to the LORD;
with all my voice I entreat the LORD.

3.   I pour out my complaint before Him;
I declare my troubles before Him

4.   when my spirit grows faint within me.
You know the course I take,
yet in the path where I walk
men have hidden a snare for me.

5.   Look^{**} to the right and see,
there is no one who takes notice of me.
I have no means of escape;
no one cares for me.

6.   I cry to You, LORD;
I say, "You are my refuge;
You are my portion in the land of the living."

7.   Listen to my cry, for I am brought very low;
rescue me from those who pursue me,
for they are too strong for me.

8.   Set me free from prison,
that I may praise Your name.
Then the righteous will gather around me,
because of Your kind dealings with me.

---

[*]   Cf. 1 Sam. 24, 3-4.
^{**} Or: 'I look'.

PSALM 143

A CALL FOR GOD'S HELP

1.   A psalm of David.

       LORD, hear my prayer,
       listen to my plea;
       in Your faithfulness and righteousness answer me.

2.   Do not enter into judgement with Your servant,
       for no man living is righteous before You.

3.   For an enemy pursues me;
       he crushes my life to the ground;
       he makes me dwell in darkness like those long dead.

4.   So my spirit is faint within me,
       my heart within me is appalled.

5.   I remember the days of long ago;
       I meditate on all Your doings;
       I reflect on the work of Your hands.

6.   I spread out my hands to You;
       my soul longs for You like a thirsty land.   *Selah*

7.   Speedily answer me, LORD,
       for my spirit fails.
       Do not hide Your face from me,
       or I shall be like those who go down into the pit.

8.   Let me hear of Your loving-kindness in the morning,
       for I put my trust in You.
       Show me the way I should take,
       for to You I lift up my soul.

9.   Rescue me, LORD, from my enemies,
       for to You I [reveal my plight, which I]
       have kept covered [from others].*

---

* Following Rashi's interpretation. Modern scholars resort to emendation.

10. Teach me to do Your will,
    for You are my God;
    let Your good spirit lead me on level ground.
11. For Your name's sake, LORD, preserve my life;
    in Your righteousness free me from distress.
12. And in Your love for me make an end of my enemies;
    destroy all who oppress me,
    for I am Your servant.

PSALM 144

A PRAYER FOR VICTORY AND PEACE

1.   Of David.

       Blessed be the LORD, my Rock,
       who trains my hands for war,
       my fingers for battle.

2.   He is my benefactor,* my fortress,
       my stronghold, and my deliverer;
       He is my shield, in whom I take refuge,
       who subdues peoples under me.

3.   LORD, what is man that You care for him,
       mortal man that You think of him?

4.   Man is like a breath,
       his days are like a passing shadow.

5.   LORD, bend Your heavens and come down;
       touch the mountains and they will pour forth smoke.

6.   Flash Your lightnings and scatter them;**
       shoot Your arrows and rout them.

7.   Reach out Your hand from on high;
       rescue me and deliver me from mighty waters,
       from the hands of foreigners,

8.   whose mouths speak lies,
       and whose right hand is raised in perjury.

9.   To You, God, I will sing a new song;
       on a ten-stringed harp I will chant praises to You,

10.   who gave victory to kings,
       who rescued His servant David from the deadly sword.

---

*   So Targum.
** i.e., the proud foes of God's people.

11.   Rescue me and deliver me
       from the hands of foreigners,
       whose mouths speak lies,
       and whose right hand is raised in perjury.

12.   When our sons are like saplings,
       carefully trained from their youth,
       and our daughters like sculptured corner columns,
       fit to adorn a palace;
13.   when our storehouses are filled to overflowing,
       affording every kind of provision;
       when our flocks increase by thousands,
       even by myriads, in our fields;
14.   when our cattle are heavily laden;*
       when there is no breaching [of our walls],
       no going into captivity,
       no cries of distress in our streets –
15.   happy are the people who have it so;
       happy are the people whose God is the LORD.

---

*   Others: 'heavy with young.'

PSALM 145

A HYMN CELEBRATING THE ATTRIBUTES OF GOD

1.   * A song of praise by David.

      I will extol You, my God and King,
      and bless Your name for ever and ever.

2.   Every day will I bless You,
      and praise Your name for ever and ever.

3.   Great is the LORD and most worthy of praise;
      His goodness no one can fathom.

4.   One generation shall laud Your works to another;
      they will declare Your mighty deeds.

5.   On the splendour of Your glorious majesty,
      and on Your marvellous deeds, I will meditate.

6.   And men shall talk of Your awe-inspiring power,
      and I will tell of Your greatness.

7.   They shall recite the record of Your abundant goodness,
      and sing joyously of Your righteousness.

8.   Gracious and compassionate is the LORD,
      slow to anger and abounding in kindness.

9.   The LORD is good to all,
      and His mercy is upon all His works.

10.   All Your works shall praise You, LORD,
      and Your devout ones shall bless You.

11.   They shall talk of the glory of Your Kingdom,
      and speak of Your might,

12.   to make known to the sons of men His mighty acts,
      and the glorious splendour of His kingship.

13.   Your Kingdom is an everlasting Kingdom,
      and Your dominion endures throughout all generations.

14.   The LORD supports all who fall,
      and raises all who are bowed down.

---

*   An alphabetical psalm, the 'nun' verse is missing.

15. The eyes of all look hopefully to You,
    and You give them their food at the proper time.
16. You open Your hand,
    and satisfy the desire of every living thing.
17. The LORD is righteous in all His ways,
    and kind in all that He does.
18. The LORD is near to all who call Him,
    to all who call Him with sincerity.
19. He fulfils the will of those who fear Him;
    He hears their cry for help and saves them.
20. The LORD watches over all who love Him,
    but all the wicked He will destroy.
21. My mouth shall declare the praise of the LORD,
    and all people shall bless His holy name
    for ever and ever.

PSALM 146

TRUST IN GOD ALONE

1.   Praise the LORD!

       Praise the LORD, O my soul.

2.   I will praise the LORD as long as I live,
       I will sing praises to my God while I exist.

3.   Put no trust in princes,
       or in mortal man who has no power to save.

4.   His spirit departs, he returns to the dust;
       on that day his plans come to nothing.

5.   Happy is he whose help is the God of Jacob,
       whose hope is in the LORD his God,

6.   maker of heaven and earth,
       the sea and all that is in them.
       It is He who keeps faith for ever.

7.   He secures justice for the oppressed,
       He gives food to the hungry.
       The LORD sets captives free,

8.   the LORD opens the eyes of the blind,
       the LORD raises those who are bowed down,
       the LORD loves the righteous.

9.   The LORD watches over the stranger;
       He gives courage to the fatherless and the widow,
       but subverts the course of the wicked.

10.   The LORD shall reign for ever,
       your God, O Zion, for all generations.

       Praise the LORD!

PSALM 147

THE WORKS OF GOD ALMIGHTY

1.   Praise the LORD!

How good it is to sing praises to our God!
How pleasant and fitting to praise Him!
2.   The LORD rebuilds Jerusalem;
He gathers in the scattered people of Israel.
3.   He heals the broken-hearted
and binds up their wounds.
4.   He counts the number of the stars
and calls each by name.
5.   Great is our LORD and mighty in power;
His wisdom is infinite.
6.   The LORD gives courage to the humble;
the wicked He brings down to the ground.

7.   Sing to the LORD a song of thanksgiving;
sing praises to our God on the harp.
8.   He covers the heavens with clouds,
provides rain for the earth,
and makes grass grow on the hills.
9.   He gives food to the cattle,
and to the young ravens when they cry.
10.   He does not delight in the strength of a horse;
He takes no pleasure in the fleetness* of a man.
11.   The LORD is pleased with those who fear Him,
with those who wait for His loving-kindness.

12.   Sing to the LORD, O Jerusalem,
praise your God, O Zion.
13.   For He has strengthened the bars of your gates;
He has blessed Your children within you.

---

*   Lit. 'thighs'.

14. He brings peace within your frontiers,
    and satisfies you with the finest wheat.

15. He sends forth His command to the earth;
    His word runs swiftly.
16. He spreads snow like fleece,
    and scatters frost like ashes.
17. He hurls down His icy hail like crumbs;
    who can stand His cold blast?
18. He issues His command and melts them;
    He stirs up His wind, and the waters flow.
19. He declared His words to Jacob,
    His statutes and rulings to Israel.
20. He has not done so for any other nation;
    of such rulings they have no knowledge.
    Praise the LORD!

PSALM 148

ALL CREATION SINGS TO THE
ALMIGHTY CREATOR

1.   Praise the LORD!

    Praise the LORD, from the heavens;
    praise Him in the heights.
2.   Praise Him, all His angels;
    praise Him, all His hosts.
3.   Praise Him, sun and moon;
    praise Him, all you shining stars.
4.   Praise Him, you highest heavens,
    and you waters that are above the heavens.
5.   Let them praise the name of the LORD,
    for He commanded and they were created.
6.   He established them for ever and ever,
    by a decree that shall never pass away.

7.   Praise the LORD, from the earth,
    you sea monsters and ocean depths;
8.   fire and hail, snow and mist,
    storm winds that obey His command;
9.   you mountains and all hills,
    fruit trees and all cedars;
10.   wild animals and all cattle,
    creeping things and winged birds;
11.   you kings of the earth and all nations,
    you princes and all judges on earth,
12.   young men, too, and maidens,
    old men and young together.
13.   Let them praise the name of the LORD,
    for His name alone is exalted;
    His majesty is above the earth and the heavens.

14.   He has exalted the renown[*] of His people,
        for the glory of all His faithful ones,
        the children of Israel, the people close to Him.

        Praise the LORD!

---

[*]   Lit. 'horn'.

PSALM 149

GLORIFY THE LORD WITH SONG AND SWORD

1.   Praise the LORD!

       Sing to the LORD a new song,
       His praise in the assembly of the faithful.

2.   Let Israel rejoice in their Maker;
       let the people of Zion exult in their King.

3.   Let them praise His name with dancing;
       and sing praises to Him with timbrel and harp.

4.   For the LORD delights in His people;
       He crowns the humble with victory.

5.   Let the faithful exult in glory;
       let them sing for joy upon their couches.

6.   Let the high praises of God be in their throats,
       and a two-edged sword in their hand;

7.   to wreak vengeance on the nations,
       punishment upon the peoples;

8.   to bind their kings in chains,
       and their nobles in fetters of iron;

9.   carrying out the judgement decreed against them.
       This is the glory of all His faithful.

       Praise the LORD!

PSALM 150

THE FINAL DOXOLOGY WITH FULL ORCHESTRA

1.   Praise the LORD!

    Praise God in His sanctuary,
    praise Him in His mighty heavens.
2.   Praise Him for His acts of power,
    praise Him according to His exceeding greatness.
3.   Praise Him with blasts of the Shofar,
    praise Him with lyre and harp.
4.   Praise Him with timbrel and dance,
    praise Him with strings and pipe.
5.   Praise Him with resounding cymbals,
    praise Him with clanging cymbals.
6.   Let everything that has breath
    praise the LORD!

    Praise the LORD!